W9-BZP-067

The gospel is God's flesh-and-blood embodiment of life-giving love. Jesus Christ is that life, the living center of that gospel. Tom Hughes is utterly convinced this Jesus alone provides the good news we all need. In *Down to Earth*, Hughes takes us into some of Jesus' most powerful stories that to this very day still invite and provoke us to find our truest and fullest life in Christ. Relish these stories and respond to Jesus' call to life—life abundant.

MARK LABBERTON, president of Fuller Theological Seminary

In *Down to Earth*, Tom highlights Jesus' use of parables throughout his ministry on earth. Tom proffers that Jesus used a parable as both a riddle and a mirror. Certainly, some parables seem straightforward, but others have always felt like a riddle to me. Through reading this book, even the ones I assumed to be straightforward have been unlocked in new ways, like riddles in sheep's clothing. What I learned through the pages of *Down to Earth* is how Jesus used parables to mirror back to us how valuable we are to him. These mirrors are meant to show us not how we see ourselves but how he sees us, as image bearers of God. Jesus not only sees us as precious but invites us to see this ourselves, as a way to step out of hiding and into deeper communion with him. Tom articulates how Jesus came not only to prove the existence of God but also to demonstrate the character and compassion of God— and he did this most powerfully through parables.

BLYTHE HILL, CEO of Dressember Foundation

Tom Hughes's book *Down to Earth* declares with great joy who God is, whose we are, and the invitation to become changed people. Tom writes and teaches with years of ministry and leadership experience, pastoring us into the stories and heart of Jesus. You won't regret reading this book that exclaims the power of the greatest story ever told!

ALBERT TATE, speaker and senior pastor of Fellowship Monrovia

The beauty of this book is that it fully lives up to its title! Tom brings heaven's stories down to earth for the here and now with real-life application, and you find yourself captivated by the Master Storyteller, Jesus, along the way.

TAMMY DUNAHOO, general supervisor of The Foursquare Church

Every one of us loves to hear a good story. We weave our own lives into its fabric as we discover that we can identify with the reality it unfolds. There is such joy in finding that in the grand stories of Jesus, there is a place for us. Let Tom Hughes guide your heart in finding yourself on the pathways of Jesus' stories that bring meaning to your life and godly perspective to living.

KEVIN MANNOIA, chaplain at Azusa Pacific University, president of International Council for Higher Education

It's one thing to tell someone that God is love; it's quite another to tell them the story of how Jesus suffered and died for them to prove that love through a beautiful song or captivating story. Jesus did the same thing when he taught two thousand years ago. He told stories. Tom Hughes has done a beautiful job of pulling out the sometimes-hard-to-understand truths of these stories in an instructive and inspiring way.

TOMMY WALKER, worship leader at Christian Assembly Church

Jesus' stories have the power to unlock the deepest realities of our lives: our regrets, disappointments, failures, and fears. Hughes helps us wrestle with these life-changing stories . . . with helpful discussion questions at the end of the book. This book contains hope and good news for all. Dig in!

DOUG SCHAUPP, national director of evangelism at InterVarsity

DOWN TO EARTH

HOW JESUS' STORIES CAN CHANGE YOUR EVERYDAY LIFE

TOM HUGHES

A NavPress resource published in alliance
with Tyndale House Publishers, Inc.

NavPress is the publishing ministry of The Navigators, an international Christian organization and leader in personal spiritual development. NavPress is committed to helping people grow spiritually and enjoy lives of meaning and hope through personal and group resources that are biblically rooted, culturally relevant, and highly practical.

For more information, visit www.NavPress.com.

Down to Earth: How Jesus' Stories Can Change Your Everyday Life

Copyright © 2019 by Tom Hughes. All rights reserved.

A NavPress resource published in alliance with Tyndale House Publishers, Inc.

NAVPRESS is a registered trademark of NavPress, The Navigators, Colorado Springs, CO. The NAVPRESS logo is a trademark of NavPress, The Navigators. *TYNDALE* is a registered trademark of Tyndale House Publishers, Inc. Absence of ® in connection with marks of NavPress or other parties does not indicate an absence of registration of those marks.

The Team: Don Pape, Publisher; David Zimmerman, Acquisitions Editor; Cara Iverson, Copy Editor; Daniel Farrell, Designer

Cover image of *The Sower* by John Everett Millais. Photography copyright © 2014 by Hyla Skopitz, the Photograph Studio, the Metropolitan Museum of Art, Rogers Fund, 1921.

Author photograph copyright © 2014 by Bob Palermini. All rights reserved.

All Scripture quotations, unless otherwise indicated, are taken from the Holy Bible, *New International Version,*® *NIV.*® Copyright © 1973, 1978, 1984, 2011 by Biblica, Inc.® Used by permission. All rights reserved worldwide. Scripture quotations marked ESV are from the ESV® Bible (The Holy Bible, English Standard Version®), copyright © 2001 by Crossway, a publishing ministry of Good News Publishers. Used by permission. All rights reserved. Scripture quotations marked NLT are taken from the *Holy Bible*, New Living Translation, copyright © 1996, 2004, 2015 by Tyndale House Foundation. Used by permission of Tyndale House Publishers, Inc., Carol Stream, Illinois 60188. All rights reserved. Scripture quotations marked NRSV are taken from the New Revised Standard Version Bible, copyright © 1989, Division of Christian Education of the National Council of the Churches of Christ in the United States of America. Used by permission. All rights reserved.

Some of the anecdotal illustrations in this book are true to life and are included with the permission of the persons involved. All other illustrations are composites of real situations, and any resemblance to people living or dead is purely coincidental.

For information about special discounts for bulk purchases, please contact Tyndale House Publishers at csresponse@tyndale.com, or call 1-800-323-9400.

Cataloging-in-Publication Data is available.

ISBN 978-1-63146-374-7

Printed in the United States of America

25   24   23   22   21   20   19
7   6   5   4   3   2   1

TO MY RADIANT BRIDE, ALLISON:

*I love you. You inspire me by the way you fiercely
and compassionately follow Jesus.*

TO MY JOYOUS CHILDREN, CALEB, SOPHIA, AND MICAH:

*May you always know that I love you, am proud
of you, and believe in you. And may you each keep
following Jesus all the days of your life.*

CONTENTS

FOREWORD *ix*

INTRODUCTION
The Greatest Stories Ever Told *xiii*

1 JESUS' MOST MISUNDERSTOOD PARABLES
The Stories of the Hidden Treasure
and the Pearl of Great Price *1*

2 A FRESH CHANCE FOR A FRESH START
The Story of Two Sons *13*

3 THE STARTLING FORGIVENESS OF GOD
The Story of the Unforgiving Servant *25*

4 THE SECRET TO A STRONGER PRAYER LIFE
The Story of the Uncaring Neighbor *39*

5 MAXIMIZING WHAT YOU'VE BEEN GIVEN
The Story of the Talents *49*

6 THE SUREFIRE WAY TO ENSURE YOUR UNHAPPINESS
The Story of the Vineyard Workers *63*

7 DOING FIRST WHAT MATTERS MOST
The Story of the Ten Bridesmaids *77*

8 THE JOY OF SPENDING SOMEONE ELSE'S MONEY
The Story of the Dishonest Manager *87*

9   WHY EVIL EXISTS NOW BUT WON'T FOREVER
    The Story of the Wheat and Weeds *99*

10 RISING HOPE IN TROUBLED TIMES
    The Stories of the Mustard Seed and the Yeast *111*

11 HOW TO BE A HERO
    The Story of the Good Samaritan *123*

12 WELCOME HOME!
    The Story of the Prodigal Son *137*

13 THE CREATIVE POTENTIAL OF A
    SOFT, DEEP, UNCLUTTERED HEART
    The Story of the Four Soils *151*

    CONCLUSION
    A Window, a Mirror, and an Invitation:
    Finishing the Stories of Jesus with Your Own Story *167*

    ACKNOWLEDGMENTS *173*

    APPENDIX
    The Parables of Jesus *175*

    QUESTIONS FOR SMALL-GROUP DISCUSSION
    AND PERSONAL REFLECTION *177*

    NOTES *185*

    ABOUT THE AUTHOR *191*

FOREWORD

WE LIVE IN THE MOST COMPLEX and volatile mixture of generations and cultures that I can ever remember. The social and political clashes being ignited by collisions of age, ethnicity, and gender are happening daily. It feels as if the world is splitting at the seams. We are witnessing meltdowns of global proportions—nations railing against each other, politicians hunkering down, families and relationships fracturing. Even our prisons are overflowing, and yet we have not stemmed the tide of pain and brokenness. There seems to be little relief in sight, and no clear leader with a solution or clarion call.

Maybe that's part of our problem: We are looking for one leader to fix it all. Just maybe, the solution lies within all of us. Perhaps the plan and pattern has already been given through the parables of Jesus, and we just need to discern it, embrace it, immerse ourselves in it, live it out, and transfer it to others. Tom Hughes has done a masterful work of compiling several of the parables of Jesus, taking extraordinary care to unpack their incredibly helpful counsel. As we come to understand and discern them, we have the chance to first find clarity about our own journey and then, second, become spokespeople for abundant life, peace, joy, grace, wisdom, kindness, and love. When an individual discovers the treasures of heaven, Tom helps us see, it not only changes their perspectives and priorities but also affects everything they influence. The rescued become the rescuer.

Jesus entered a world of institutional, political, and religious oppression. The delicately balanced systems of people were often the sources of the world's problems, rather than pathways to solutions. Their focus was hinged solely on authority and obedience. Collisions abounded everywhere back then too. But Jesus began to shift that thinking. He highlighted godly values, not organizations or rules, as the pathway to elevate people above their problems. In human-made systems, people are often treated as objects to be used, leveraged, and manipulated. But Jesus saw people as objects of his affection to be restored and helped at every turn. His parables demonstrate the value he places on every person, and they hold keys to help people navigate life.

Tom Hughes is like a tour guide through Jesus' parables, pointing out the things that are often missed because of our poor vantage point or lack of insight or experience. That's the focus Tom takes throughout his life. He is an unconventional leader (in the best sense) whom I've grown to admire and respect. He puts others first. He is less concerned about protocol and more concerned about people and principles. His leadership is breaking hard ground, breaking through difficult situations where it's been hard to imagine hopeful or helpful possibilities. He has one hand on Jesus' teaching, and with the other hand, he is reaching out to connect us to this lifeline. People are being rescued and are becoming rescuers.

You only do that when your values align with Christ's and

when you deeply care about the future of others. In this book, Tom has marshaled the forces of heaven to combat the forces of darkness. *Down to Earth* has the possibility of releasing people from their personal places of imprisonment—some there by their own decisions, others by being pulled along into the conforming culture of a fallen world. As Tom points out, Jesus doesn't spend a lot of time on how we got to where we are; instead, Jesus focuses his words and stories on how to get going in the right direction, how to anticipate and avoid the danger spots, and how to help others do the same.

The church is indebted to Tom Hughes for his tenacious focus, energy, and work to unpack the stories of Jesus. The powerfully healing, releasing, and empowering truths in this book will unleash heaven's resources, bring clarity to places of confusion, rescue those derailed by their own decisions or the situations they find themselves in, help stem the tide of the dangerous forces of evil, and initiate a resurrection effect in every arena that desperately needs life breathed over it. And just maybe, our story will become a bridge to the greatest story ever told.

Glenn Burris Jr.
PRESIDENT, THE FOURSQUARE CHURCH

THE GREATEST STORIES EVER TOLD

The shortest distance between a human being and the truth is a story.

ANTHONY DE MELLO

THE STORIES JESUS TOLD ARE the greatest stories ever told.

That's a bold claim in a world filled with stories. If it's true, then this book is worth your time to read. Let me see if I can back it up.

Jesus was a master storyteller. It's been estimated that up to a third of his teachings came in the form of stories (often called parables) about the Kingdom of God. If you want to know Jesus or understand God's Kingdom, then you have to wrestle with the parables of Jesus.

I say *wrestle* rather than simply *read* or *hear* because that is the point of the parables. They are not just stories to be heard; they are riddles to be unlocked. In fact, the Hebrew word for parable means just that: a riddle.[1] The Greek word for parable means "to throw alongside."[2] Like a farmer throwing seed on soil, Jesus is not just telling stories; he is "throwing riddles alongside." Alongside what? Another story: ours.

In considering these riddles, viewpoint is everything. A theologian once told of a time when he held his infant son up in front of a mirror. The baby moved; the reflection moved. The baby waved; the reflection waved. Suddenly the youngster's face lit up. He realized, "That's me!"[3]

That is how these riddles work. The parables begin as black print on a white page. Told long ago in a faraway place, they seem to be irrelevant to our day and time. But as Jesus tells them, the time and space seem to disappear. On the pages of Scripture, you see a reflection of yourself and an invitation to join in and live in the Kingdom of God. They are the greatest stories of all time not only because of who told them but also because they have the power to change us.

If these stories are the greatest ever told, we would expect to see that they have stood the test of time—that they are resilient and relevant across cultures and generations. And, in fact, that is what we see. They have inspired people to create some of the most beautiful art ever created: paintings, sculptures, stained-glass windows, poems, and songs ranging from hymns and symphonies to rap and rock. References to the parables of Jesus are everywhere.

It's not just art. Countless hospitals are named Good Samaritan. Every time you hear of a talent show, you are hearing the echo of one of the parables of Jesus. And most people, including those who have never read Jesus' actual parables, know that a prodigal-son story is one of loss and redemption.

The parables of Jesus were always drawn from daily life. They are stories about fathers and sons, farmers and seed, business agreements and fishing trips, baking and banquets. They have been called earthly stories with heavenly meanings, but that can be misleading, suggesting that they have nothing to do with the here and now. It is more on target to say that they challenge us to join in with God's work in our everyday lives.

Jesus' stories connect us to him. We are told that "Jesus used many similar stories and illustrations to teach the people as much as they could understand" (Mark 4:33, NLT). Apparently, Jesus knew that we are wired *for* stories and can be rewired *by* stories. Recent brain-scan studies show that stories influence our thoughts; moreover, the mere act of storytelling cultivates a relationship between the storyteller and listener.[4] The closer the connection, the greater the listener's understanding of not only the story but also the storyteller.

The more we understand Jesus' stories, the closer we will be to him. Likewise, the closer we desire to be with him, the more we will understand what he is saying through his stories. It's a virtuous cycle. As Jesus observed, "Whoever has will be given more, and they will have an abundance" (Matthew 13:12). However, for those with hearts hardened toward him, the parables might never move beyond being merely interesting stories (see verse 15).

Jesus' parables require us to think, pray, wrestle, and do some soul-searching as these down-to-earth stories give us a view into how the Kingdom of God operates. When we do these things, not only do we see the Kingdom of God, but like the baby in the mirror, the stories help us see ourselves and the condition of our own hearts in light of the stories Jesus tells. Our understanding and our hearts are tied together.

Yet when Jesus' disciples asked him about the parables that they did not understand, he explained everything to them (see Mark 4:34): They could discover the purpose of the parable by simply asking Jesus. Thankfully, we have not only the parables of Jesus but also some of his explanations recorded afterward.

The parables are concise, with intriguing plots usually involving crises of some sort. They always include a surprise from what we may have initially expected. By the end of the stories, we are always left to issue verdicts. However, the point of these verdicts is not to simply say the right answer; it's to live the right answer. The stories do not end when Jesus finishes telling them. They continue in our own lives as we grow, change, and do life differently because of them.

Jesus' parables were almost always told to groups of people. At the end of the book, you will find a section with questions for each chapter. You can use these to guide your own personal reflection. Even better, I invite you to use this book with a small group to grapple with the parables together as Jesus' original listeners did. We will be considering fifteen of Jesus' parables, but you can find a list of twenty-nine of them at the end of the book to further your growth in following Jesus.

So come with me as we take a look at some of these riddles that Jesus throws alongside our lives so we can better understand and live out this thing called the Kingdom of God. These down-to-earth stories not only hold the power to entertain, intrigue, and make us curious but also have the power to help us clearly see and know God, make a fresh start, set priorities, forgive, maximize our talents, cope with evil and suffering, and love others well.

They are not just stories to be heard; they are stories to be continued. The parables of Jesus come to us with surprising twists and different perceptions to teach, challenge, convict, heal, comfort, and motivate us. They are the greatest stories ever told because they hold the power to change the world. In fact, they already have. But they are not done. Now these down-to-earth stories have come to change *your* world too.

CHAPTER 1

JESUS' MOST MISUNDERSTOOD PARABLES

The Stories of the Hidden Treasure and the Pearl of Great Price

Nowadays people know the price of everything and the value of nothing.

OSCAR WILDE

The Son of Man came to seek and save those who are lost.

JESUS (LUKE 19:10, NLT)

IT FEELS AS IF WHAT SOMETHING is worth is constantly up for grabs. Not long ago, I was in the process of purchasing airline tickets for an upcoming trip, and the price changed while I was in the process of booking them! And, of course, the price went up, not down. Then a week later, after I'd already purchased tickets, an email alerted me to the fact that the same flight, same day, same airline had now dropped in price (again with no price guarantee).

It's not just airline tickets. The "in" toy from last year isn't so "in" anymore. The brand-new car driven off the lot immediately loses value. A company's valuation on the stock exchange can change from moment to moment.

How can we know what something is actually worth?

It's a question we face every day. On one hand, we can confuse something that has only temporary value with something that is of lasting value. On the other hand, there are times when we recognize what is of real value—what is very good and truly valuable—and we organize our lives around those things.

Jesus tells two parallel stories back to back as a way of emphasizing that we are constantly faced with the challenge of deciding what something is worth. How you understand these two stories influences how you understand yourself, God, and living your one and only life. I believe that the following two parables are the most misinterpreted of Jesus' parables. See if you agree.

WHAT IS WORTH WHAT: BEGIN AT THE BEGINNING

[Speaking to his disciples, Jesus said,] "The Kingdom of Heaven is like a treasure that a man discovered hidden in a field. In his excitement, he hid it again and sold everything he owned to get enough money to buy the field.

"Again, the Kingdom of Heaven is like a merchant on the lookout for choice pearls. When he discovered a pearl of great value, he sold everything he owned and bought it!"
MATTHEW 13:44-46 (NLT)

The standard interpretation of these two parables is that we are like the man in the first story or the merchant in the second one. We find the treasure that is the Kingdom of Heaven. Seeing that it is of such great value, we give our all to buy it. We are the one doing the seeking, the finding, and the purchasing. We are the hero in the story.

But is that really what Jesus is trying to tell us? Maybe.

But maybe not.

"Am I the man or the treasure?" "Am I the merchant or the pearl?" Before we wrestle with the ends of the stories, we have to wrestle with their beginnings. We have to ask ourselves, "Who is what?"

Just prior to the parables, Matthew tells us,

> Jesus always used stories and illustrations like these when speaking to the crowds. In fact, he never spoke to them without using such parables. This fulfilled what God had spoken through the prophet:
>
> "I will speak to you in parables.
> I will explain *things hidden since the creation of the world.*"
>
> MATTHEW 13:34-35 (NLT), EMPHASIS ADDED

If these parables are about "things hidden since the creation of the world," determining who is what in these parables requires us to go back to the creation of the world:

> God said, "Let us make humankind in our image, according to our likeness; and let them have dominion over the fish of the sea, and over the birds of the air, and over the cattle, and over all the wild animals of the earth, and over every creeping thing that creeps upon the earth."
>
> So God created humankind in his image,
> in the image of God he created them;
> male and female he created them. . . .
>
> God saw everything that he had made, and indeed, it was very good.
>
> GENESIS 1:26-27, 31 (NRSV), EMPHASIS ADDED

The Hebrew word that is translated *good* can also be translated as *precious, valuable, excellent,* and *pleasing.*[1] Genesis tells us that for the first five days of creation, at the end of each day's work the creation was good. However, here at the end of the sixth day's work of creation, the day that God made people in his image, it was *very good.* In other words, Genesis is underlining the value that God saw when he considered the people he had created. All of creation was good, except those beings made in God's image—they were *very good.*

Living in a global marketplace, we can absorb the illusion that value is determined by "What have you done for me lately?" We often extend that way of thinking to ourselves, measuring our worth based on grades, job reviews, number of social-media followers, or amount of money in our bank accounts. We slip into thinking that our value is determined by how others feel about us or even how we feel about ourselves. That might work well on our good days, but what about on our bad ones?

Genesis offers us a different picture. Humans are created on the sixth day. The people had not even done anything yet. They had not produced or created or even multiplied. And day seven was set apart as a day of rest—the very first full day of human existence was a day of rest.

Our being called very precious and valuable before we had done anything and then given a day of rest to start our experience of life underscores that our value must be intrinsic to who we are, not just what we do.

THE SOURCE OF OUR VALUE

God declares us very valuable, but where does this value come from? It comes from the fact that you and I were created in the image of God. Authentic image gives and determines value. God does not make any counterfeit human beings.

The value of a US hundred-dollar bill is not based on where it has been or how it has been used. Its value is not determined by its shape, size, or color. A one-dollar bill in American currency has the same shape, size, and color as a hundred-dollar bill. If you want to know what the bill is worth, what matters is whose image is on it. George Washington's image tells us that it is a one-dollar bill we are holding. If we have a bill with the image of Benjamin Franklin, then we know we are holding a hundred-dollar bill. How do you determine what *you* are worth?

You need to know whose image you bear.

So here's what is true about you: Regardless of whether things are going well or not, whether you feel great or glum, because you were created in the image of God, you are of the highest value.

This can be a challenge for some of us to accept because the things around us have constantly changing values.

The thing is, you are not a thing.

According to Matthew, the prophecy said that the Messiah will "explain things hidden since the creation of the world." Then Jesus tells a parable about a hidden treasure and then another one about a pearl. We've seen that God has given us great value, but where does the hidden part come into play?

In Genesis 3, we learn that Adam and Eve let fear and skepticism take root in their hearts. Up to this point, they had experienced only good. However, the enemy of God tempts them to believe that the Creator is not planning for their best interest. So they eat of the tree of the knowledge of good and evil.

It's essential to note that the Hebrew word translated *knowledge* carries with it a sense of experience. It's not just that Adam and Eve were intellectually aware of evil's existence; it's that by becoming skeptical of God's nature and purposes and intentions for them, they opened themselves to the experience of evil. Here's what we are told:

> The man and his wife heard the sound of the LORD God as he was walking in the garden in the cool of the day, and they *hid* from the LORD God among the trees of the garden. But the LORD God called to the man, "Where are you?"
>
> He answered, "I heard you in the garden, and I was afraid because I was naked; *so I hid.*"
>
> GENESIS 3:8-10, EMPHASIS ADDED

God gave us the highest value by making us in his image, but when he comes looking for us, our totally false perception of him causes us to hide ourselves from him. God's plan of sharing his joy with the creatures of his affection—created in his image and dearly precious to him—is challenged by our propensity to doubt that love. How could God's reputation be renewed and light be shed on the now dark, worrisome, and skeptical place in the human soul? How could that happen, and what would it cost? In other words, what is worth what?

THE FOUR STAGES OF LOVE

About a thousand years after Jesus told these two parables, a monk named Bernard of Clairvaux wrote something that has helped shine some light on these parables for me. Clairvaux founded seventy monasteries and observed a four-stage development in a person's relationship with God. See if you can find yourself at any of these stages as a way of moving forward in your relationship with God.[2]

The first stage is the love of ourself for the sake of ourself. We all start here. We are concerned for only ourself, aware of only our own needs. As babies we have no choice but to begin our lives in an entirely self-centered reality. But we don't have to stay there.

The second stage is the love of God for the sake of ourself. We step into loving God but only on the basis of what he can do for us. Clairvaux noted that this is as far as most people ever travel in their lives. One way to tell if this is where we are is to listen to our prayers. If our prayers mainly consist of asking God to give us something or protect us from something or make something happen for us, we are probably at this second stage. If this is where our love for God stops, we are in danger of hating God if he does not give us what we want when we want it.

The third stage is the love of God for the sake of God. This is where we begin to sense that God has value simply because of who he is. Just as he declared that we have value simply because of who we are, we now can make that same declaration about him. Just as he valued us before we had done anything, we can now value him also for who he is.

This is the beginning of joy and wonder for many people. God did not have to be the way he is. He did not have to create animals as wonderful and weird as the platypus, but he did. He did not have to make sunsets so majestic and beautiful to us, but he did. God's character does not have to be filled with mercy, creativity, generosity, and grace, but it is. That such a God does exist becomes the point of delight and joy.

When I first read these stages, I thought that this third one should be the end of it. If we could each get over ourself long enough to love

God solely for who he is, that should be the top of the mountain, right? But I was surprised to read about the fourth stage.

According to Clairvaux, the fourth stage is the love of ourself for the sake of God. When I first read this, it rubbed me the wrong way. It seemed selfish, prideful, and arrogant. It seemed to be a great step backward, not forward. And then I thought about how being a pastor serving in the most diverse neighborhood in Los Angeles means that I have had the privilege of sitting with many different people: men and women of seemingly every ethnicity and background imaginable, some exceedingly rich and others exceedingly poor, some very young and some very old. I have learned that it is very rare to find a person who does not suffer from some level of blatant self-dislike or even self-hatred.

Some people focus on physical traits, desiring to be taller or thinner or to look different than they do. Others are introverts wanting to be extroverts (or vice versa). Still others wish they had different natural skills or abilities: "If only I could write music like she does"; "If only I could speak as well as he does"; "If only I could build a business like my friend." Some people seem to think that God did not really know what he was doing when he created them. If you have ever struggled with negative feelings toward yourself, it is a surprising discovery to find out how God feels about you. This fourth stage is when we have caught a vision of the value he has placed within us.

Which brings us back to these two parables that Jesus told of the hidden treasure and pearl.

WHAT IS SOMETHING REALLY WORTH?

What is a thing worth? It's worth what someone is willing to pay for it.

In Jesus' other parables that have a person searching for something that is hidden, covered, or lost, God is not who is hidden or lost; we are. Just like in Genesis. God is the one doing the searching. This fits exactly with Jesus' understanding of himself: "The Son of Man came to seek and save those who are lost" (Luke 19:10, NLT). God is a seeker.

Christ sees our value in spite of all of the broken, messy, value-distorting fears and sin we have covered ourselves in. He sets aside his divine privileges (sounds like a man who "sells" everything) and takes the form of a baby in a manger. Skepticism had set into the human soul from Genesis 3, but in Luke 1:68, interestingly, we are told that God has *epeskepsato* us.

Many English Bibles translate *epeskepsato* as "visited."[3] It's an unfortunately bland translation, as it obscures the lightning of what is happening in Jesus' coming down to earth.

Epe means to move toward someone or something with helpful intent. *Skepsato* is where we get our English word *skeptic*. Putting it together, when Jesus came, he "moved toward the skeptics with helpful intent."[4] Who are the skeptics? As we just saw in Genesis, me and you. And what are we skeptical of? God's good character, intentions, and plans for us.

And so we hid from God, and Jesus came from heaven to seek and save what was lost. He who set aside his divine rights to visit the skeptics with helpful intent did this by eventually dying on the cross (see Philippians 2:7-8).

He did this all for the joy that was set before him (see Hebrews 12:2). What does that joy consist of? A restoration of the unbroken communion that we were created to have with God from the creation of the world—a treasure that was once hidden and lost and is now being found again.

Most people have at least some time in their lives where they struggle with issues of self-worth or wonder how God sees them. Whether that happens a lot in your life or only episodically, God declares that you are worth the coming of his Son, Jesus Christ, who arrived in a manger to be with us. Zephaniah says it this way:

> The LORD your God is living among you.
> He is a mighty savior.
> He will take delight in you with gladness.
> With his love, he will calm all your fears.
> He will rejoice over you with joyful songs.
>
> ZEPHANIAH 3:17 (NLT)

With Jesus' arrival in the manger, the Father declared, "You are worth it!"

THE TREASURE IN THE DIRT IS STILL VALUABLE

And now we ask, "But what about my sin? My messed-up life? My addiction? My secrets? Don't those remove my value to God? Just because I once was of great value and great worth does not mean that I still am."

Don't believe that lie about yourself and about God.

Think of it this way. How much is a crisp, clean hundred-dollar bill worth? A hundred dollars. How much is a dirty, crumpled, hidden hundred-dollar bill worth? A hundred dollars. Why? The image might be in need of restoration and cleansing, but it is still there. While we were still in the dirt of sin, in the fear of evil, in the anger, in the isolation we covered ourselves with, God not only came looking for us but came to pay the highest price for us: "He was pierced

10

for our rebellion, crushed for our sins. He was beaten so we could be whole. He was whipped so we could be healed" (Isaiah 53:5, NLT).

On the cross, Jesus was the man and the merchant who sold everything he had in order to pay for the treasure that had been hidden, the pearl of great price to him. In Christ, you were "bought with a price" (see Acts 20:28; 1 Corinthians 6:20; 7:23; 2 Peter 2:1). God's Word is clear that the mystery of this Good News is now available to all who would hear and respond by faith (see Romans 16:25-26; 1 Corinthians 2:7; Ephesians 3:7; Colossians 1:26). If you respond by placing your faith in Jesus and follow him, that is what it means to be "in Christ."

In the book of Revelation, the city of God is described. It contains twelve gates. On the gates are written the names of the twelve tribes of Israel, and each of the gates is made of a single pearl (see 21:9-21).

A pearl is unique among all the precious stones in creation because it is the only precious stone that is created through pain. It is the result of a grain of sand creating pain within a clam, which then secretes a fluid that hardens around the grain of sand. When we see a pearl, we see something that has been made lovely through the process of pain. That is the very story of the gospel of Jesus. We are forgiven and are being healed, renewed, and restored, but it happened through the process of his freely entering into the pain of the Cross on our behalf. What God thinks you're worth is clear and unwavering: You are worth everything to him.

RESPONDING TO GOD'S LOVE

What has been paid for us is of greater value than anything that will ever be asked of us. If indeed, within these parables, we are the pearl and the treasure as opposed to the merchant and the man, it frees us to embrace and live from God's assessment of our great value and preciousness to him. It calls us out of our tendency to hide and out of our feelings of worthlessness. Even in your hiddenness and sin, Jesus Christ has judged you to be worth his everything. "God demonstrates his own love for us in this: While we were still sinners, Christ died for us" (Romans 5:8). This is Good News. This is the gospel.

No longer are we forced to live lives in which our value rises and falls based on grades, jobs, social-media likes and followers, or any other external circumstances. This gritty story invites us to live in the joy of the stability of a value that comes from the fact that we were created in the image of God. Faith is not just believing in God; it is believing that he is good. Faith rejects the skepticism that says that God is in it only for himself. The Cross is God's ultimate rejection of the enemy's lie from the beginning that God is really only about himself. Faith sees that we do not do things hoping to prove our worth to him or earn his love. Faith sees that we already have it.

Life, then, is not an attempt to earn God's love. Instead, his love is the fuel and the power to live the lives we were created to live. In other words, we are pearls of great price. And thanks be to God that he was willing to pay it so we could be freed from our hiddenness and sin, restored to life with the one who loves us from the very beginning.

So then the question becomes "How do I handle regrets in my life? Can God redeem the things I wish I'd done differently?" Well, Jesus once told a story about that, which we will look at next.

CHAPTER 2

A FRESH CHANCE FOR A FRESH START

The Story of Two Sons

There are only two kinds of people: the righteous who think they
are sinners and the sinners who think they are righteous.

BLAISE PASCAL

God specializes in giving people a fresh start.

RICK WARREN

BACK IN 1958, a baby boy was born into the Lane family. The
father, a man named Robert, chose to name his boy Winner. How
could the young man fail to succeed with a name like *Winner Lane*?

Several years passed and the Lanes had another son. For unknown
reasons (this is a true story), Robert named this boy Loser. How
tragic to doom the boy's future prospects with the name Loser Lane.
How many counseling sessions did it take to undo that?

Of course, all the family's friends thought they knew how the
two boys' lives would unfold. But contrary to all expectations,
Loser Lane succeeded. He graduated from college and later became
a sergeant with the NYPD, shield number 2762. Nowadays, no
one feels comfortable calling him Loser. His colleagues simply
refer to him as Lou.

And what of the brother with the can't-miss name?

The most noteworthy achievement of Winner Lane is the sheer length of his criminal record. Inmate number 00R2807 has nearly three dozen arrests for burglary, domestic violence, trespassing, resisting arrest, and other mayhem.[1] Sometimes things are not as they first seem.

Jesus once told a parable about a different father and two sons. In fact, what many people do not know is that Jesus actually told two different parables about a father and two sons. The more famous story (the parable of the prodigal son, which we'll get to later in the book) has inspired everyone from Rembrandt, who painted about it, to Imagine Dragons, who sang about it.[2] This is Jesus' *other* story about a father and two sons. It may be less famous but is no less potent in changing our daily experiences as we live out its meaning.

Jesus was teaching at the temple one day, when some leading priests and elders interrupted him. In the ensuing conversation, Jesus told them this story:

> "What do you think about this? A man with two sons told the older boy, 'Son, go out and work in the vineyard today.' The son answered, 'No, I won't go,' but later he changed his mind and went anyway. Then the father told the other son, 'You go,' and he said, 'Yes, sir, I will.' But he didn't go.
>
> "Which of the two obeyed his father?"
>
> They replied, "The first."
>
> MATTHEW 21:28-31 (NLT)

This short but powerful parable is told in two acts. One of the sons seems like a winner from the start, and one seems like a loser from the start.

ACT ONE

Dad and his two sons are sitting around the breakfast table. In those days, family life and work life were intimately connected. Sons worked for their dads, so the dad giving instructions for the day's work is to be expected.

He tells son #1 to go and work in the vineyard. This son has a mind of his own. Wearing torn jeans and vaping an e-cigarette, he looks up from his half-eaten bowl of Froot Loops and says, "You must be kidding. The vineyard is hard work and long hours: bend, pull, carry, and sweat. No, thanks. That's not for me."

The tension at the breakfast table is thick. This is a strikingly rude response for a son to make to his father. The father turns to son #2 and tells him to go and work in the vineyard. This son is wearing Dockers, a button-down Oxford, and deck shoes and is eating a tofu omelet.

Have you ever observed that when one sibling gets in trouble, the other becomes sickeningly good?

The second son says, "Yes, sir, I will go." He is cheerful and compliant. He lays it on thick. "Dad, the vineyard would be my highest honor. It may not be to some, but for me it is an utter privilege. Thank you for asking me. I was thinking in my morning devotions, 'I so love the vineyard.'" Dad and Mom beam as they watch their second son. He's the hero of the family. The curtain drops on act one.

ACT TWO

Son #1 slams the door, jumps on his Harley with his girlfriend, and rides off. But a strange thing happens: As he is cruising away to the syncopated roar of the engine, he cannot get his dad's words out of his head. He thinks of all that his father has done for him, thinks about the honest state of his own life. His heart softens and his stubbornness melts. The word Jesus uses here means to have a change of mind—to turn around.

So he drives his Harley to the vineyard to the shock of his dad, who never expected this son to show up. The father turns to share his joy with son #2. But son #2 never actually shows up at the vineyard. So cheerful, so compliant—no harsh words, but now it's clear he never intended to work at all. Not all rebellion is outward.

He wasn't smoking, but it's clear now that he was blowing smoke.

Two sons: one openly defiant to the will of the Father but has a change of heart; the other saying the right words but not following through with action. Jesus asks, "Which of these two did the will of the father?" The original listeners correctly answer, "The son who went to the vineyard."[3]

THE GOD OF FRESH STARTS: SEAN'S STORY

God is still in the business of welcoming to his vineyard people who originally wanted nothing to do with him. My friend Sean is one of them. He was raised in a home with parents who were very supportive and caring, but God was not part of the family home. His parents taught him that working hard and being an achiever is how you are spotted and get ahead in life. Sean is a natural athlete. He played baseball, football, and soccer. He graduated from high school with honors and had high hopes of playing baseball in college. However, in college Sean was exposed to many things that he was not prepared to handle. I'll let him tell his story in his own words:

In college I was very discouraged that I was not noticed by the coaches for my hard work on the baseball field. Along with that, there was a lot of partying and drug use going on around me in the dorms where I lived. I joined a fraternity. It was there that I was introduced to the world of hard drugs. What started with alcohol and marijuana turned to cocaine, mushrooms, and LSD. I found myself spiraling into this world of not caring about anything except where I would get the next high.

After years of drug abuse, I ended up in Las Vegas working in construction and running with the wrong crowd. One morning after being up for a couple of days, I was in a room with a group of friends, trying to recover. I was in and out of sleep and had this vision of being above the room and looking down on all of us, and I heard an audible voice say, "Is this where you want to be in ten years?" It was so clear to me, and my answer was no.

I decided to move away from Las Vegas and start over but quickly learned that my habits had followed me home. I continued to party and get into trouble, and one night I decided to drop acid with a few friends. It was the worst experience of my life. I had this clear feeling that I was going to die and that there was no hope for me. At one point I dropped down on my knees and confessed my sins to another guy who was there. I felt so strongly that I needed forgiveness. That night as I lay in my bed, I still had the feeling that I was going to die, and I had no idea what I was going to tell God about how I had lived my life. I had no excuse, and I was so afraid to face God. I felt very strongly that there was a war going on for my soul that night. In my desperation, I cried out to God that if he would let me make it through the night, I would try to know him.

The next morning, I woke up and felt different. I tried to get high, but something was different. It tasted different, it felt different, and I did not want it anymore. I quit everything cold turkey. I didn't know how to "know" God, but my mom had a very large heirloom Bible that I would randomly open to a verse and, after reading it, feel that I was good for the day.

I had a long commute to my new job each day, and I stumbled upon a pastor on the radio talking about God in a way that I had never heard before. He talked about how an intimate relationship with God was available and said that I could be forgiven of my sin and set free from the bondage of slavery. I wanted that, and during one of the invitations to accept Christ as my savior, I gave my heart to God on the 405 freeway. I later called the phone number for the radio ministry and said that I had given my life to Christ. The ministry sent me a new-believer's growth packet, which included a New Testament and a guide for my next steps, and I have never looked back.[4]

For all of the Seans of the world, Jesus' parable of the two sons shines a lot of assurance and freedom onto our dark and confining pasts. Here's the truth of this parable: What was true of you back then doesn't have to define you now.

FRESH CHANCE FOR A FRESH START

THIS IS NOT A BREAKFAST PARABLE

The son who was a pain at breakfast turns out to be a joy at dinner. The son who was a joy at breakfast turns out to be a pain at dinner. Unfortunately for the second son, this is a dinner parable, not a breakfast parable. What matters is where you are when dinner comes.

There's both a warning and an encouragement here. The warning is that simply talking a good game or starting out well is not enough. The encouragement is for those of us who have said and done things we regret, and we fear we will never be able to live down our pasts or be forgiven for them. Good endings can come from bad beginnings.

God is more interested in your present decision than in your past failures. Why? Because what was true of you back then does not have to control you now. That is the gift of the God-given power to make a change. When the initially rebellious son shows up at the vineyard, the father does not chastise him about the earlier conversation; he welcomes him to do the father's will. The Father still welcomes anyone who comes to do the Father's will, regardless of the individual's past.

In his explanation of this parable, Jesus alludes to an earlier time when John the Baptist taught about the right way to live. Here's how Luke records that day:

> Even corrupt tax collectors came to be baptized and
> asked, "Teacher, what should we do?"
>
> [John] replied, "Collect no more taxes than the
> government requires."
>
> "What should we do?" asked some soldiers.

John replied, "Don't extort money or make false accusations. And be content with your pay.'"

LUKE 3:12-14 (NLT)

Notice in those responses that more than being assured that they were baptized for the forgiveness of their past sins, these people wanted to know how to now live out their new faith in their regular lives. In these instances, the examples are not people leaving their jobs but rather doing their jobs in a different, more Kingdom-minded way.

Needless to say, some occupations are simply incompatible with living out the Kingdom of God. That's why I don't think we are given an example of John instructing prostitutes on ethical ways to sell their bodies. Sometimes walking into the future God has freed you for includes walking away from the past systems and actions that imprisoned you. A number of years ago, I met a guy I will call Richard. He had recently decided to make a commitment to follow Christ. However, the problem was that he produced pornography for a living. His question was, "What should I do?"

In the end, he rightly concluded that he needed to quit his job and leave his past work behind him. To his credit, he did just that. There is no godly way to make pornography and sell it. He let go of his past and walked into his new future. And God provided other, more purposeful work. What was true of him back then does not define him now.

FRESH STARTS AND NEW CHOICES

Maybe you need to hear the bright side of this parable: that the father does not hold the breakfast conversation against the son who said he would not go to the vineyard but ultimately does choose to go there. Maybe your past was filled with hating your neighbor, but with God's help you've changed. Maybe your past was envy, lust, and rage, but now, with God's help, you've changed. Maybe you always poisoned your relationships with gossip, but with God's help you've changed. If you've turned from your sin and confessed it to the Lord and he's forgiven you, then you no longer have to hold it against yourself. You are free. Remember, what was true of you back then doesn't have to define and control you now.

This parable is about the power to change, but more deeply, it's about actions that come from authentic belief. True belief leads to believing action. When Jesus explains the parable to the leading priests and elders to whom he tells it, he says,

> John the Baptist came and showed you the right way to live, but you didn't believe him, while tax collectors and prostitutes did. And even when you saw this happening, you refused to believe him and repent of your sins.
>
> MATTHEW 21:32 (NLT)

Notice that Jesus says that John showed them the right way to live. Belief leads to being shown not just an old way to leave behind but also a new way to grab hold of and live out. Danish philosopher Søren Kierkegaard once observed,

> People try to persuade us that the objections against Christianity spring from doubt. That is a complete misunderstanding. The objections against Christianity spring from insubordination, the dislike of obedience, rebellion against all authority. As a result people have

21

hitherto been beating the air in their struggle against objections, because they have fought intellectually with doubt instead of fighting morally with rebellion.[5]

In the case of the leading priests and elders, they did not believe, so they did not change their actions; the tax collectors and prostitutes believed, so they did change their actions. Belief and actions must always be connected or else we might just be kidding ourselves about what we really believe.

GETTING IN THE WHEELBARROW

One of my favorite stories of revealing authentic belief is the story of Charles Blondin, the French tightrope walker. On June 30, 1859, he did his most famous act when he became the first person to cross a tightrope stretched across the mighty Niagara Falls. The tightrope was more than a quarter mile long, suspended 160 feet above the falls, and he walked across several times, each time in a different way: once on stilts, once on a bike, once in the dark, and once blindfolded!

A large crowd gathered to watch, with each feat bringing louder applause. At a different performance, the crowd oohed and aahed as Blondin carefully walked across, one dangerous step after another, pushing a wheelbarrow holding a huge sack of potatoes. Then at one point, he asked the crowd, "Do you believe I can carry a person across in this wheelbarrow?"

The crowd enthusiastically yelled, "Yes! Yes! We believe! You are the greatest tightrope walker in the world. We believe!"

"Okay," said Blondin, "who wants to get into the wheelbarrow?"

They said they believed, but no one was willing to get into the wheelbarrow.[6]

This parable of the two sons is not an idle story that Jesus told to create curiosity in us; it is a mirror meant to help us reflect on our own stories, our own lives. Maybe the reflection you see in Jesus' parable is an area where you are not now in the vineyard. Maybe you have patterns of deceit in your life that God wants to free you from. Or perhaps you have addictive patterns, pride, or sexual sin. Maybe you know that God is calling you to figure out what is true about him but you keep making excuses or letting less important things fill your time. In what area is God calling you to get to the vineyard, trusting that his will for you is good?

The choice is yours. You can say, "Yes, God. Do your work in me. I'll stop resisting, evading, denying, pretending, and procrastinating." Or you can resist, as the first son in the parable does. You can harden your heart and dig in your heels. You can tell yourself that you will go to the vineyard another day but not today. If you are resisting God, it is dangerous and expensive, but you can choose to change your mind, because this is a dinner parable, not a breakfast parable.

Of course, there is also the danger of being the second son. Like him, we can offer superficial compliance but never follow through with true believing action. The second son wants the appearance and approval of obedience without the hard work of obeying. He wants to be known as a person of faith and belief without ever being willing to get into the wheelbarrow.

Let me go back to my friend Sean—the addict who came to Jesus on a bad acid trip. He didn't grow up in a family of faith in Jesus. With God's help, he was able to leave his addictive past behind him. When he first walked into a church building, he felt certain he did not belong—that it would cave in on him. He has now been clean and sober for nineteen years. What used to control him and define him no longer has that power over him. With Sean, not only does his past not define him, but God has built this beautiful redemption of his past. Sean is now the leader of our welcome and hospitality teams at the church I serve.

The forgiveness of Sean is majestic and something only God can do, yet it goes beyond that. Not only does God forgive, but in some kind of divine alchemy, he can take the most painful parts of our past and use them for good. In Sean's case, the one who feared he could never be welcomed because of his past is now one of our most visible welcomers of others. Sean is literally a living, breathing, walking, smiling, down-to-earth story for all who meet him and are wondering if it is really possible to move beyond our pasts into the good futures God has in store for us. It is.

Just ask Sean.

CHAPTER 3

THE STARTLING FORGIVENESS OF GOD

The Story of the Unforgiving Servant

A man that studieth revenge keeps his own wounds green.

FRANCIS BACON

Everyone thinks forgiveness is a lovely idea,
until they have something to forgive.

C. S. LEWIS

WHEN SHANNON ETHRIDGE WAS just sixteen years old, an act of forgiveness and love changed her life forever.

Driving to her high school one morning, Shannon struck and ran over Marjorie Jarstfer, who was riding her bicycle along a country road. Marjorie died, and Shannon was found completely at fault by the authorities. Consumed by intense guilt, she contemplated suicide several times, but she never took her life, because of the healing response of one man: Gary Jarstfer.

Gary, Marjorie's husband, forgave the sixteen-year-old and asked the attorney to drop all charges against her. This saved her from an almost certain guilty verdict. Instead, he simply asked Shannon to continue in the godly footsteps that his wife had taken. "You can't let this ruin your life," Gary told her more than thirty years ago. "God wants to strengthen you. In fact, I am passing Marjorie's legacy on to you."

Gary's act of forgiveness showed Shannon the amazing restorative love of God. That act became the foundation of her work seeking to help people overcome guilt-ridden, wounded lives.[1] Sometimes our greatest misery can become the foundation of our greatest ministry.

DEALING WITH HURTS AND LOSS

The truth is that we cannot live in this world very long without being hurt. Maybe your story is as dramatic as Gary's tragic loss of his wife and his choice to forgive. However, your story does not have to rise to that level of loss for you to experience real pain in our sin-riddled world. As a pastor, I have heard countless stories from people of how they have been wounded, mistreated, or victimized. There is so much betrayal and pain, injustice and pure evil, that has happened to students, young adults, senior citizens, men and women, and people of every ethnicity. It seems that no one is immune. It is heartbreaking.

How do we handle it when someone has wounded us?

This is not a new question. It has been around as long as people have been around. One way to respond is as a man named Lamech did: "I have killed a man for wounding me, a young man for injuring me. If Cain is avenged seven times, then Lamech seventy-seven times" (Genesis 4:23-24). The rule of Lamech is not to do only what they have done to you; it's to do worse. It's not just revenge; it's revenge many times over. Lamech was wounded, so he killed the young man for causing the injury.

Most of us would not go that far, but we can certainly be

THE STARTLING FORGIVENESS OF GOD

tempted to do damage to those who have hurt us. Even if we cannot always exact actual revenge, our hearts can stew in resentment and bitterness toward the person who created the wounds.

Jesus had a story to tell about the nature of forgiveness that alluded to the rule of Lamech. Jesus' disciple Peter asked, "Lord, how many times shall I forgive my brother or sister who sins against me? Up to seven times?" (Matthew 18:21). Peter had already heard Jesus teach that forgiving others is a necessity (see 6:12, 14-15), but the practical matter occurs as to the limits of how often a person is to be forgiven. The consensus rabbinic teaching of the day was to forgive someone up to three times and then after that you could seek revenge.

Jesus answered, "I tell you, not seven times, but seventy-seven times" (18:22). Peter must have thought he was being generous by stretching the rabbinic teaching to seven times. Jesus goes far beyond that. He turns the rule of Lamech inside out. Instead of seeking vengeance seventy-seven times, the pathway forward in life is the way of maximum forgiveness.

But how is that even possible?

A PARABLE OF ASTOUNDING
AND DISTURBING FORGIVENESS

Jesus goes on to tell this story:

> The kingdom of heaven is like a king who wanted to settle accounts with his servants. As he began the settlement, a man who owed him ten thousand bags of gold was brought to him. Since he was not able to pay, the master ordered that he and his wife and his children and all that he had be sold to repay the debt.

At this the servant fell on his knees before him. "Be patient with me," he begged, "and I will pay back everything." The servant's master took pity on him, canceled the debt and let him go.

But when that servant went out, he found one of his fellow servants who owed him a hundred silver coins. He grabbed him and began to choke him. "Pay back what you owe me!" he demanded.

His fellow servant fell to his knees and begged him, "Be patient with me, and I will pay it back."

But he refused. Instead, he went off and had the man thrown into prison until he could pay the debt. When the other servants saw what had happened, they were outraged and went and told their master everything that had happened.

Then the master called the servant in. "You wicked servant," he said, "I canceled all that debt of yours because you begged me to. Shouldn't you have had mercy on your fellow servant just as I had on you?" In anger his master handed him over to the jailers to be tortured, until he should pay back all he owed.

This is how my heavenly Father will treat each of you unless you forgive your brother or sister from your heart.

MATTHEW 18:23-35

Anytime you discuss forgiveness, it is important to clarify what forgiveness is not. Forgiveness is not excusing. Some actions are excusable and do not require forgiveness. If you are seated near a mother with a fussy baby on an airplane ride, she may offer you an apology out of politeness for the disruption. You may *feel* sinned against, but people share space, and babies fuss. The reasonable response calls not for forgiveness but for simple kindness and understanding toward the mother. You probably fussed when you were a baby too.

Forgiveness is also not forgetting. It is not a form of spiritual amnesia. In the parable, the king remembered that he had given the servant forgiveness. Forgiveness requires that we are aware of what happened and yet choose to extend mercy anyway.

And forgiveness is not necessarily reconciliation. It may very well pave the way for reconciliation, but in some cases the person is not even present any longer. For example, I have sat with people who have come to forgive someone who has died, and, of course, reconciliation was not possible. In cases in which the offending person is still alive or available, reconciliation requires acknowledgment and repentance on the part of the offending person. However, that does not always happen. Just because someone has sinned does not mean the individual will own his or her responsibility. Prior to this parable, Jesus addresses how to handle this immediately:

> If your brother or sister sins, go and point out their
> fault, just between the two of you. If they listen to you,
> you have won them over. But if they will not listen, take
> one or two others along, so that "every matter may be
> established by the testimony of two or three witnesses."
> If they still refuse to listen, tell it to the church; and if
> they refuse to listen even to the church, treat them as
> you would a pagan or a tax collector.
>
> MATTHEW 18:15-17

Jesus makes it clear here that forgiveness is not tolerance. Among his community, his instructions are not to simply tolerate it when someone sins against you. Instead, we are told to confront it directly and graciously. That may lead to repentance and seeking forgiveness; however, that is not guaranteed, which is why Jesus explains how to handle the situation with escalating steps of severity.

Reconciliation may not always be possible, because reconciliation requires both parties to want to rebuild trust and goodwill. As a friend once observed, "It takes two people to reconcile, but it takes only one person to forgive." The person you are forgiving may not want that, and you cannot force it from them. And although confession and repentance often make forgiveness easier, it is not always a prerequisite for forgiving someone. As Jesus said from the cross, "Father, forgive them, for they do not know what they are doing" (Luke 23:34).

A STARTLING AMOUNT OF DEBT

The disciples hearing this parable of the unforgiving servant would have been startled at the amount of money the servant owed the king. The actual word Jesus uses is a "talent," which was the equivalent of about twenty years' wages for a laborer. So then ten thousand talents would require two hundred thousand years to pay back! It is equivalent to about $7 billion today.[2] There was simply no hope whatsoever of being able to repay the debt. In ancient times, debtors had both their property sold for cash and their family members sold into servitude to try to recoup some of the loss (see 2 Kings 4:1; Nehemiah 5:3-5; Isaiah 50:1; Amos 2:6; 8:6). Although the servant asks for patience, he gets something better than patience from the king: mercy and forgiveness. But it is critical to note that the mercy costs the king. It is not free. It costs him ten thousand talents to grant the servant mercy.

German pastor Dietrich Bonhoeffer, who died at the hands of the Nazis, once said that "all forgiveness is a form of suffering."[3] Either it will be suffering by the other person in the form of our vengeance, or it will become suffering by us in the form of forgiveness. For example, let's imagine that a friend borrows your car. While driving it, he or she runs into a light post, disabling the car's engine. One of two things will happen: Either you will make the person pay, or you will forgive the debt. But in the case of the forgiveness, what happens to the car? Either you will have to pay for the repairs yourself, or you will have to pay the price of the inconvenience of walking everywhere. Once the event has happened, a debt never just vanishes—someone always ends up paying.

Many of the wrongs we have suffered are much more serious than a disabled car. The truth is that maybe someone attacked us, robbed us of opportunities, or took something from us that we simply can't get back. If that has happened to you, let me say that I am so very sorry that happened to you. It is heartbreaking to hear so many people's stories of real pain and loss. Not all wrongs can simply be undone. Some debts cannot be repaid by those who committed them. Maybe your spouse had an affair or someone said words that cannot just be erased from your memory. It creates a debt and that person owes you.

When those moments come in life, you can try to make the other person pay by destroying his reputation and opportunities. You can secretly hope he suffers; you can work to remove opportunities for him, exacting revenge; or you can forgive him. This last one is hard because it requires you to deny yourself. Depending on what the situation is, it can be a form of agony. It's part of what I think Jesus had in mind when he told his followers to pick up their crosses and follow him. Very few of us will have to carry literal crosses. Many of us will have the choice to suffer so that another can be forgiven.

FORGIVENESS PAYABLE
TWENTY-FIVE CENTS AT A TIME

In Jesus' story, the forgiven servant goes out a free man. His $7 billion debt has been forgiven. It cost the king, but it was free for the servant. The forgiven servant then encounters a man who owes him one hundred denarii, which would be the equivalent of about twelve thousand dollars.[4] On its own, this is certainly not an inconsequential amount; however, compared to the $7 billion that had just been forgiven, it is. The forgiven servant now hears the exact same plea for patience. However, instead of forgiving the man, he chooses to make him pay.

The servant had promised the king he would "pay back everything" (Matthew 18:26), but he flat-out refuses to pay forward any of the mercy he received from the king. Paying forward the startling grace and mercy that God gives us is a logical and expected response. But although we might imagine that we do so in some grand gesture, paying forward mercy is more of an ethic in our daily lives than a big onetime event. Professor and pastor Fred Craddock once observed,

> We think giving our all to the Lord is like taking a $1,000 bill and laying it on the table: "Here's my life, Lord. I'm giving it all."

But the reality for most of us is that he sends us to the bank and has us cash in the $1,000 for quarters. We go through life putting out 25 cents here and 50 cents there. . . . Usually giving our life to Christ isn't glorious. It's done in all those little acts of love, 25 cents at a time.[5]

The actions of the servant are brought to the attention of the king. The servant's unwillingness to pay the mercy forward, even for such a lesser amount, shows that he had not truly been influenced by the king's startling mercy. Maybe the gratitude for his own forgiveness had worn off. Maybe it was never present to begin with. Maybe he thought he was entitled to the king's forgiveness. Entitlement is always the enemy of gratitude.

Some commentators on this parable try to find a way around the king's action of handing over the unmerciful servant to the jailers. They feel it is too harsh for him to revoke his initial act of mercy. To me, it seems quite fair within the story; however, it becomes much more disturbing when I move it from the servant's story to my own story. That's the genius and power of Jesus' stories: they hold the power to change our lives because they get past our usual self-justifying defenses.

As disturbing as the master's retraction may be, it is consistent with Jesus' other words on forgiveness. For example, he teaches his disciples to pray that our Father will "forgive us our debts, as we also have forgiven our debtors" (Matthew 6:12). He goes on to say, "For if you forgive other people when they sin against you, your heavenly Father will also forgive you. But if you do not forgive others their sins, your Father will not forgive your sins" (verses 14-15). As New Testament scholar N. T. Wright astutely observes, "Indeed, throughout the New Testament we are constantly warned that the choices we make in this life, especially the choices about what sort of person we might become, are real and have lasting consequences which God himself will honor."[6] Jesus' parable drives home the point that when it comes to forgiveness, "what has been done to us, must be done by us,"[7] as noted by theologian Miroslav Volf.

In other words, forgiven people are to forgive people.

Forgiveness can happen in a moment of time, or it can be a journey over time. It is one thing to say the words "I forgive you"; it is quite another to actually forgive from the heart. Sometimes our hearts need to catch up with what we know is true. The fact is that we have a bigger debt before God than anyone else has before us. Jesus' story makes it clear that remembering the size of our debt creates the power to forgive not just three times or even seven times but countless times.

A DOWN-TO-EARTH STORY OF REAL-LIFE FORGIVENESS

It is fair to ask if this gritty story about the servants can stand up to our down-to-earth real-world tragedies. It's nice as a parable, but is it powerful in our everyday lives? Consider what happened to Mary Johnson. On February 12, 1993, Mary's only son, twenty-year-old Laramiun Byrd, was murdered by a sixteen-year-old named Oshea Israel. Mary said that she hated Oshea.

She said, "Here was I, a Christian woman, full of hatred. I was pleased he was going to be tried as an adult for first degree murder. . . . In court I viewed Oshea as an animal and the only thing that kept me going was being able to give my victim impact statement. I was inspired by my faith, and so I ended off by saying I'd forgiven Oshea 'because the Bible tells us to forgive.' When Oshea's mother gave her statement she asked us to forgive him, and I thought I had. But I hadn't actually forgiven. The root of bitterness ran deep, anger had set in and I hated everyone. I remained like this for years, driving many people away."[8]

God eventually impressed upon Mary that she needed to visit Oshea in jail. They met for two hours, and for the first time, Mary could see that Oshea was genuinely sorry for what he had done. It was at that meeting that Mary genuinely forgave him. For his part, Oshea could not believe that Mary could do this. He was stunned and asked if he could hug her.

So they hugged.

Mary continues, "When he left the room I bent over saying, 'I've just hugged the man who'd murdered my son.' . . . From that day on I haven't felt any hatred, animosity or anger. It was over."[9]

Oshea was released from prison, having served seventeen of the twenty-five-year sentence. He now lives back in the old neighborhood; in fact, he lives next door to Mary in their apartment building. Mary was actually the person who introduced Oshea to her landlord. With Mary's permission, the landlord invited Oshea to move into the building. Mary even threw Oshea a "welcome home" party. Mary is clear that forgiving Oshea does not excuse or diminish what he did. However, as a Christian who had received God's forgiveness in her life, she felt compelled to try to pay that forgiveness forward into Oshea's life.

Oshea has now turned his life around. He and Mary now spend much of their time on an organization they created that is dedicated to ending violence through healing between families of victims and those who have caused the harm. Oshea says that he is still working on the process of forgiving himself for what he did. He says, "I have learn[ed] that if you hold on to pain it grows and grows but if you forgive you start to starve that pain and it dies."[10] And Mary sings the line "I am so grateful, Lord, for all that you have done for me." It is that gratitude for all the Lord has done that compels her to pay forward the mercy she could never pay back.

SOMEONE HAS TO PAY, AND SOMEONE ALREADY HAS

Jesus' parables are not pointless stories; they help us understand the down-to-earth reality of God's Kingdom and invite us to enter into that Kingdom.

Once a debt is created, someone must pay. Jesus told the story of the king who forgave the massive debt. And then he turned that part of the parable into part of his life. He absorbed that massive debt onto himself by dying on the cross. It is this fact that answers the last part of the forgiveness process. When we are wronged, we instinctively want someone other than ourselves to pay for the injustice.

The cross of Jesus shows us that someone already has.

When we choose to bear the cost of forgiveness, we find Christ nearby, as he has also borne that cost for us and with us. He knows how we feel. He bears the weight with us not only for what has been done to us but also for what we have done to others. Our debt creates his suffering; his grace motivates him to bear it. That is why he said that he must suffer (see Luke 9:22). By absorbing the costs of all sins onto himself, Jesus creates the possibility for the end of retaliations. He creates the possibility for such stories as those of Mary Johnson and Oshea Israel, and Gary Jarstfer and Shannon Ethridge. He creates possibilities for *your* story of forgiveness too. Maybe as the forgiven one. Maybe as the forgiver. Probably both in different stories throughout your life.

N. T. Wright once recounted a famous story of an archbishop who shared about three hardened teenagers who decided as a joke to go into the confessional at the local church and confess all kinds of outrageous sins that they claimed they had committed. The priest was no fool and saw through their gag quickly. The first two of the students ran out of the church laughing, but the priest challenged the third one. He said to the remaining teenager,

> "Okay, you have confessed these sins. I want you to do a penance. I want you to walk up to the far end of the church and I want you to look at the picture of Jesus hanging on the cross, and I want you to look at his face and say, 'You did all that for me and I don't care that much.' And I want you to do that three times."
>
> And so the boy went up to the front, looked at the picture of Jesus and said, "You did all that for me and I don't care that much." And then he said it again, but then he couldn't say it the third time because he broke down in tears. And the archbishop telling the story said, the reason I know that story is that I was that young man. There is something about the cross. Something about Jesus dying there for us which leaps over all the theoretical discussions, all the possibilities of how we explain it this way or that way and it grasps us. And when we are grasped by it, somehow we have a sense that what is grasping us is the love of God.[11]

We forgive not because we feel like it or it is easy; we forgive because it is necessary. We forgive because we are forgiven our startling debt before our Master by what Christ did through the Cross and Resurrection. So as we face those who seek our forgiveness, we are empowered to forgive them when we remember the unpayable debt that has been forgiven us. It is in choosing to forgive others that we reveal that God's forgiveness really transforms us. It is also the way for us to pay forward a relatively small portion of debt that we could never pay back.

CHAPTER 4

THE SECRET TO A STRONGER PRAYER LIFE

The Story of the Uncaring Neighbor

> Any concern too small to be turned into a prayer
> is too small to be made into a burden.
>
> **CORRIE TEN BOOM**

> Don't worry about anything; instead, pray about everything.
> Tell God what you need, and thank him for all he has done.
>
> **PHILIPPIANS 4:6 (NLT)**

ACCORDING TO SOCIOLOGICAL STUDIES, what do Americans do on a daily basis more often than go to work?

Pray.[1]

Prayer is not only something that happens often in our lives; it's also something that increases significantly as we grow older. It's not just that older people pray more than younger people, although that is true; it's that the *same people* pray more as they age. Compared to when they were polled in their twenties, roughly a third more Baby Boomers as well as a third more Gen Xers now report praying daily.[2] So whether you are young and pray daily or are aging and discerning that you are more drawn to prayer as you get older, you are not alone.

One day Jesus was praying. When he finished, one of his

followers said to him, "Lord, teach us to pray" (Luke 11:1). It's interesting that he did not say, "You don't need to be taught to pray. You just pray. Just talk to God. You can't get it wrong. Anyway, all prayers are the same. All prayers are acceptable."

Instead, Jesus effectively said, "Okay, I'll teach you about prayer." And he had some very specific things to say about prayer. He taught us how to pray and told a story that we need to understand to know the secret of a better prayer life.

A PRAYER WITH NO I'S, ME'S, OR MY'S

Jesus said [to his followers], "This is how you should pray:

"Father, may your name be kept holy.
  May your Kingdom come soon.
Give us each day the food we need,
and forgive us our sins,
  as we forgive those who sin against us.
And don't let us yield to temptation."

LUKE 11:2-4 (NLT)

If you have heard this prayer before, you might be thinking, *Wait a minute, Jesus. You didn't say it right. You have the "Father" in there but forgot the "who is in heaven." You got the "may your Kingdom come soon," but forgot "your will be done on earth as it is in heaven." Jesus, you misquoted your own prayer! That is weird, isn't it?*

Luke is recounting Jesus' prayer here on a different occasion from the more commonly known version that was recorded by Matthew. Jesus is doing what many teachers of that day did: giving the shorthand version of the prayer he had already taught his followers before he gets to the story he wants to tell them to change their perspective and practice of prayer.

It is interesting to observe that you can pray the entire prayer without saying *I*, *me*, or *my*. The American culture elevates the individual above all else, yet when teaching us to pray, Jesus taught a communal prayer, with plural pronouns that begin with "our Father and his Kingdom," not "me and my Kingdom."

It is not that our needs don't get addressed. Our needs are included throughout the prayer: our need for daily bread, our need to forgive and be forgiven, and our need to not yield to temptation. They are all named but in the context of coming to God as our providing Father.

Growing up, I had a great dad. Not perfect, but great in my eyes. He was present and caring and provided for us through his hard work, he loved to laugh, and he told me every day that he loved me, was proud of me, and believed in me. I hope that was your experience with your dad too. However, maybe you had a different experience. Maybe your dad was begrudging, unwelcoming, absent, or even worse. Jesus knew that we would need help understanding the heart of our heavenly Father, which is why he goes on in his teaching on prayer to tell us a story. It starts out as a story about a neighbor but ends up being a story about our heavenly Father.

HOW DOES GOD EXPERIENCE OUR PRAYERS?

Teaching them more about prayer, he used this story: "Suppose you went to a friend's house at midnight, wanting to borrow three loaves of bread. You say to him, 'A friend of mine has just arrived for a visit, and I have nothing for him to eat.' And suppose he calls out from his bedroom, 'Don't bother me. The door is locked for the night, and my family and I are all in bed. I can't help you.' But I tell you this—though he won't do it for friendship's sake, if you keep knocking long enough, he will get up and give you whatever you need because of your shameless persistence.

"And so I tell you, keep on asking, and you will receive what you ask for. Keep on seeking, and you will find. Keep on knocking, and the door will be opened to you. For everyone who asks, receives. Everyone who seeks, finds. And to everyone who knocks, the door will be opened."

LUKE 11:5-10 (NLT)

Everyone listening would have been familiar with this situation. Hospitality in Jesus' day was a much higher value than for us in our culture. When traveling, there were no places to stop for food or rest—no Chick-fil-A, no Best Western. Giving and receiving hospitality was essential for survival. Due to the heat of the day in Jesus' part of the world, the accepted practice was to start your traveling in the evening, often arriving at your destination late into the night.

In the story, the guest arrives when the daily bread has all been eaten. The host is not adequately prepared to feed him, so the host goes to a neighbor. He asks for three loaves of bread—a modest request. He is trusting in the generosity of his neighbor, and to be asked was an honor. Nowadays, when our neighbors' houses are all battened down for the night, we assume the kids are asleep and we do not dare wake them.

This is the point Jesus wants to make: "Can you even *imagine* that happening?" Everyone said, "No way! Unthinkable! Impossible!" For many modern readers, we might think this is acceptable. However, to all of Jesus' first listeners, each excuse was ludicrous. We can slip into seeing ancient people as inherently inferior compared to today, but such reflexive thinking has rightly been called "chronological snobbery."[3] It's worth considering what we have lost in our connection with our neighbor by outsourcing hospitality to an industry rather than it being a cultural norm.

But Jesus effectively says, "Pretend with me for a while that it happened. What would you do next? You would stay at the door and keep knocking every five minutes so the guy cannot go to sleep. He will eventually say to his wife, 'Is he still at the door?' At last he will respond. Friendship will not move him, but your persistent disturbance will."

This is where many of us can get the wrong idea. We may think, *Oh, okay. I get it. God is like the cranky neighbor. But if you keep banging on the door, you might bother him enough that he will give you what you want so you will leave him alone.* That's what the pagans believed about prayer. The Greek and Roman gods were indifferent toward people. So the cultural belief was that in order to get something from them, you would have to wear them down by disturbing them to the point where they give up out of annoyance.

That is exactly *not* what Jesus is saying by this story.

WHAT GOD IS *NOT* LIKE

The neighbor is not the mirror image of God; in fact, God is the opposite of the neighbor. This is a story of contrast, not likeness.

If you think this is a story of likeness, then you will completely misunderstand the heart of prayer and the heart of God that Jesus came down to earth to reveal to us. You'll think that Jesus is saying that even if your neighbor is grouchy and set against you, you can wear him down by disturbing him so you can get what you need and then go away.

We know that this cannot be what Jesus means for us to take from this story. We know this because elsewhere when he teaches on the topic of prayer, he explicitly says, "When you pray, don't babble on and on as the Gentiles do. They think their prayers are answered merely by repeating their words again and again. Don't be like them, for your Father knows exactly what you need even before you ask him!" (Matthew 6:7-8, NLT).

What Jesus is communicating is that if this is true with an unimaginable neighbor, *how much more* should you confidently ask and pursue our Father, who never sleeps, is eager to give, is never distant, and is closer than your next breath. This parable is classified as a "how much more" parable, which ancient rabbis often used. Those parables were always ones of contrast. The uncaring neighbor is bothered by the disturbance; because of God's great care for us, God is not bothered and doesn't consider our requests a disturbance.

If we took everything we are grateful for and every problem we are worried about to God first, it would do wonders in terms of our connection to him throughout our day. There was an English revivalist with a great last name: Smith Wigglesworth. Here's what he said: "I don't ever pray any longer than twenty minutes. . . . But I never go twenty minutes without praying."[4] If we think of God as the cranky neighbor, we will be hesitant to go to him in prayer. But if we see that Jesus is telling a story of contrast, not likeness, then our lives will become infused with prayer. Getting the point of this parable right is the secret to a better prayer life.

BETTER THAN THE NICEST NEIGHBOR

Jesus is committed to making sure that we don't misinterpret the story, so what starts out as a story about an irritable neighbor is finished with Jesus speaking about the over-the-top, loving Father.

> You fathers—if your children ask for a fish, do you give them a snake instead? Or if they ask for an egg, do you give them a scorpion? Of course not! So if you sinful people know how to give good gifts to your children, how much more will your heavenly Father give the Holy Spirit to those who ask him.
>
> LUKE 11:11-13 (NLT)

Not only is God not a grumpy neighbor, but he is not even a nice neighbor. For those in Christ, he is our loving Father (see John 1:12-13). A fish is scaly like a snake. A scorpion balled up might be initially mistaken for the shape of an egg. However, what dad would disguise food for the evil pleasure of plotting to harm his young children? That's not normal even among us fallen people. Like God, parents love to give good gifts to their children.

A few weeks ago, I was in a little beach town in California called Cayucos. I told my kids to jump in the car because we needed to go somewhere. They grumbled some, as kids can do. "Why do we have to go somewhere? Where are we going, anyway? I'm too tired to go anywhere."

But all that disappeared when I pulled up in front of the Brown Butter Cookie Company. I told them they could each pick out a big cookie. Undeniably, I love chocolate chip cookies, but what I love even more is giving the good gift of fresh, warm, soft chocolate chip cookies to my children.

My youngest son took a bite of the chocolate chunk cookie and said, "I think I just discovered what glory tastes like." I did not even know that he had ever heard of the word *glory*, let alone knew it had a taste! If we being imperfect still long to give good gifts to our children, then *how much more* will our perfect heavenly Father give good gifts to us.

The disciples wanted to know the secret to Jesus' strong prayer life. Through this story, Jesus is showing us that the secret to a better prayer life is rightly seeing that God is our good father who desires to give us good gifts. In God, there is no annoyance at requests to him from us; there is only goodness and generosity. That is who God is. So keep coming and do not quit praying.

Now the truth is, we may get disappointed when we pray. Some prayers seem to go unanswered and we do not understand why. Not all of our prayers will be answered immediately. Sometimes when the unthinkable happens and there are no answers to why, we do well to pray for a peace that surpasses understanding that God's Word tells us is available to us (see Philippians 4:6-7).

WHY DO WE KEEP COMING BACK TO PRAYER?

Immediately upon finishing this story, Jesus says, "And so I tell you, keep on asking, and you will receive what you ask for. Keep on seeking, and you will find. Keep on knocking, and the door will be opened to you. For everyone who asks, receives. Everyone who seeks, finds. And to everyone who knocks, the door will be opened" (Luke 11:9-10, NLT).

The question naturally surfaces that if God is a loving Father who desires to give to us, why do we need to keep on asking? Keep on knocking? Keep on seeking? Why not just ask once and receive it? Maybe God really does want us to bang down the door as the pagans used to try to do for their supposed gods. Doesn't that interpretation fit these words of Jesus better?

Remember the context of this story. Jesus told this story in direct connection with the prayer he taught his disciples to pray. When we see the story through that lens, it becomes clear why we are told to keep on asking, knocking, and seeking.

How often do we need daily bread? Every day. We keep asking because our needs keep arising anew. How often do we need forgiveness and to forgive? Regularly. How often do we face evil and need deliverance? Constantly.

We don't keep asking because our needs are never met; we keep asking because even as the daily needs are met by God, they arise again the next day. What Jesus is saying is that we can be confident to keep asking because such a humble appeal to our loving Father will work again and again since he is not like the cranky neighbor who gives out of annoyance. God is the generous Father, who delights to keep meeting our needs as they arise. He's not one and done.

We may wonder why he did not create the world in such a way that our needs are met once and for all time. As a father, I think the reason for that is our Father will meet our needs but desires more than for only our needs to be met; he desires a relationship with us. Prayer is an essential part of that relationship.

A GIFT BETTER THAN FISH AND EGGS

Jesus finishes this teaching on prayer with an unexpected turn: After talking about dads who give their children the good gifts of a fish or egg to eat, he says, "So if you sinful people know how to give good gifts to your children, how much more will your heavenly Father give . . ." (Luke 11:13, NLT).

And this is where everyone expects Jesus to say, "Good gifts such as fish and eggs when you need them." But that is not what Jesus actually says. Here is how he finishes that sentence: "How much more will your heavenly Father give *the Holy Spirit to those who ask him*" (verse 13, NLT, emphasis added).

In other words, our Father is so good that we do not have to reluctantly wear him down. We are persistent in our prayers because our needs are persistent in recurrence. God welcomes us, unlike the touchy neighbor. He is such a good Father that he not only gives us what we need like daily provisions but will give us his very Spirit if we ask him. If you have never asked God to give you the Holy Spirit, I encourage you to do that now, trusting that he will answer that request. Sometimes we become concerned with debating Jesus' words rather than simply obeying them.

Author John Claypool once told of the impact on his life of a woman he knew growing up. Her name was Gladys Meggs. John noticed that she was always cheerful and full of life. As a little boy, he asked her why she was always like that no matter what was going on in her life.

She responded, "Ain't nothing going to happen today that me and Jesus can't handle!"[5]

That is the exact mind-set this down-to-earth story was meant to give us.

CHAPTER 5

MAXIMIZING WHAT YOU'VE BEEN GIVEN

The Story of the Talents

Nothing is more common than unfulfilled potential.

HOWARD HENDRICKS

It is within my power either to serve God or not to serve Him. Serving Him,
I add to my own good and the good of the whole world. Not serving Him,
I forfeit my own good and deprive the world of that good,
which was in my power to create.

LEO TOLSTOY

CHUCK YEAGER, the famed test pilot of old, was flying an
F-86 Sabre over a lake in the Sierras when he decided to buzz a
friend's house. During a slow roll, he suddenly felt his aileron lock.
Says Yeager, "It was a hairy moment, flying about 150 feet off the
ground and upside down."[1] A lesser pilot might have panicked
with fatal results, but Yeager let off on the G's and pushed up the
nose, and sure enough, the aileron unlocked.

Climbing to a safer height, Yeager tried the maneuver again.
Every time he rolled, the problem reoccurred. Yeager knew that a
few pilots had died under similar circumstances, and investigators
had been unable to find the Sabre's fatal flaw. After his incident,
Yeager went to the investigators with a report, and from that they
found that a bolt on the aileron cylinder was installed upside down.

Eventually, the culprit was found in a North American plant. He was an older man on the assembly line who ignored instructions about how to insert that bolt because he'd assumed that all the bolts were designed to be placed head up, not head down. Yeager said that nobody ever told the man how many pilots he had killed.[2]

An odd common thread in humans is our attempts to avoid, charm, or explain our way out of the consequences of our actions. We become masters of shifting the blame, always believing that someone else is responsible for our lives. And when we ignore the instruction for God's plan for our lives, untold others suffer the consequences of our decisions. On the other hand, when we decide to pursue God's plan with a sense of divine urgency, not only do we become the beneficiaries, but so do those around us. As the band the Red Hot Chili Peppers sings, "This life is more than just a read-through."[3] There is one to whom we will give an account of our life, and there will be no finessing our way around him.

To help us see this truth, Jesus tells what has become one of his more famous stories:

It will be like a man going on a journey, who called his servants and entrusted his wealth to them. To one he gave five bags of gold, to another two bags, and to another one bag, each according to his ability. Then he went on his journey. The man who had received five bags of gold went at once and put his money to work and gained five bags more. So also, the one with two bags of gold gained two more. But the man who had received one bag went off, dug a hole in the ground and hid his master's money.

After a long time the master of those servants returned and settled accounts with them. The man who had received five bags of gold brought the other five. "Master," he said, "you entrusted me with five bags of gold. See, I have gained five more."

His master replied, "Well done, good and faithful servant! You have been faithful with a few things; I will put you in charge of many things. Come and share your master's happiness!"

The man with two bags of gold also came. "Master," he said, "you entrusted me with two bags of gold; see, I have gained two more."

His master replied, "Well done, good and faithful servant! You have been faithful with a few things; I will put you in charge of many things. Come and share your master's happiness!"

Then the man who had received one bag of gold came. "Master," he said, "I knew that you are a hard man, harvesting where you have not sown and gathering where you have not scattered seed. So I was afraid and went out and hid your gold in the ground. See, here is what belongs to you."

His master replied, "You wicked, lazy servant! So you knew that I harvest where I have not sown and gather where I have not scattered seed? Well then, you should have put my money on deposit with the bankers, so that when I returned I would have received it back with interest.

"So take the bag of gold from him and give it to the one who has ten bags. For whoever has will be given more, and they will have an abundance. Whoever does not have, even what they have will be taken from them. And throw that worthless servant outside, into the darkness, where there will be weeping and gnashing of teeth."

MATTHEW 25:14-30

THE GOD WHO TRUSTS YOU

In Jesus' day, there were no corporations as we know them. Wealth was concentrated in the hands of a few rich households, and this household was one of them. The owner gathers three employees and then something extraordinary happens: he delegates all his wealth to them.

The master's generosity is unprecedented. A talent in Jesus' day was originally a unit of measurement of money. As already mentioned, it was equivalent to twenty years' pay for the average worker. In today's economy, a talent would be worth about seven hundred thousand dollars. Even the person trusted with a single talent is receiving an exceptional gift to manage.

This parable has become so well known to English-speaking people that the word *talent* has now come to mean any gift that is given to a person by God. When reading the word *talent*, you can insert all that you have been given by God: your life, your time, the finances under your care, your mind, your will, and all your opportunities.

One of the central attributes of God is that he is a giver: "God so loved the world that he gave . . ." (John 3:16). It dawns on the servants that they have a once-in-a-lifetime chance. This is an opportunity to show themselves to be trustworthy and faithful—to exercise initiative and jump in with both feet. By the end of the parable, we see that those who manage their talents appropriately also get to share in the abundance generated (see Matthew 25:29) as well as share in the joy of the master (see verses 21 and 23). For a servant to rise to such a position of significant responsibility and opportunity as well as share in the profits was unheard of in Jesus' day.

This gift is their defining moment. How will they respond?

Two servants go immediately with a sense of urgency to each do his best with what he has been entrusted with. They realized that they would be insane to let anything stand between them and this chance of a lifetime. In a very real sense, your life is a lifelong chance of a lifetime. All of it is a gift from the Master. None of it comes from you. As novelist and poet Robert Louis Stevenson saw, "Nothing but God's Grace! We walk upon it; we breathe it; we live and die by it; it makes the nails and axles of the universe."[4]

Jesus tells this story about ordinary human beings who can jump in and be of use in the Kingdom of God. Two of the servants did just that. Jesus' point is not for you to discover what the servants in the story do with their talents; it is to cause you to think about what you will do in your story with your talents. It's a story of normal people being given the opportunity to make a real difference in the Kingdom of God. Jesus tells us this parable because this offer is still open today. He's still looking for those kinds of people today.

In the story, everyone has talents. There are no "no talent" people in the beginning of the story. God has given you at least one talent. You must come to prize what the Lord of the gift has given to you. Are you ready to fully invest, or are you waiting for a better offer, a bigger stage, or a more prestigious platform? Don't wait.

God will never hold us accountable for talents he has not given us. Focus on the talents of others and you will bury the talent that has been given to only you. He will never ask you why you did not live someone else's life or why you did not use someone's talents. He will, however, ask you what you did with what he gave you. Did you jump in with passion to serve his good purposes, or did you stay on the sidelines?

If there ever was a person who you would think had a reason to sit on the sidelines of life, it is Nick Vujicic. Nick was born in 1982 in Melbourne, Australia, with no arms or legs. His condition is called phocomelia, and there is no known medical, genetic, or environmental reason for it. He has credited his faith in God for the power to overcome the initial question of why he was born the way he was, as well as the loneliness and depression that initially marked his life.[5]

Instead of focusing on what he lacks, Nick has made the most of what he has been given: a sharp mind, a winsome personality, and the ability to be a compelling speaker. The doors have opened for Nick to share the news of Jesus everywhere, from Oprah Winfrey's talk show to the Kremlin. At a recent event, Nick said,

> God the Father is calling the followers of Jesus to be the hands and feet of Jesus. I know that might sound weird coming from a man who has no hands and no feet! But if God can use me to be his hands and feet to help others, then he can use any willing soul.[6]

Nick is clearly a man who takes seriously Jesus' story about making the most of what each of us has been given.

THE RESPONSIBILITY OF GOD'S GENEROSITY

In the parable, the owner departs for a long time, but not forever. When the Master returns, all accounts will be settled. Generosity and accountability are not mutually exclusive. What do we do in the in-between time of encounters with the Master once we have been given such an abundant gift? We make a *response* to our God-given *ability*. We can even see that in the word *responsibility*.

The first two servants had different gifts but the same reward: a share in the abundance as well as an invitation to enter into the joy of the master. The third servant's situation is where things turn ugly. It's interesting that unlike the first and second servants, the third servant does not begin with a reference to the amount with which he had been entrusted. He does not remember or acknowledge the master's generosity. Forgetfulness often leads to fearfulness. When we forget all that God has done for us, we fear what he is like and what the future may bring.

The master holds the third servant accountable for a sin of omission: knowing the good he should have done but choosing not to do it. Sin is not always something we do; it can also be the good within our power to do that we intentionally leave undone (see James 4:17). The underlying issue is that the third servant wants to evade accountability for his life.

"Don't blame me," he says. "My inactivity is rooted in my view of your character." The master does not defend himself or even contradict the servant. He does not say, "You misread me." He doesn't say, "Whether you use your talent or not does not really matter to me. I see you are upset, and this feels like pressure. My primary goal is to spare you any discomfort, so let's just pretend I never even brought this up."

When the third servant accuses the master of being a hard man, he has closed his heart to the master's initial act of generosity. He claims to know that the master is a hard man, but what is clear is that he never really knew the master's character at all. He claims that the master reaps where he has not sown—in essence, that the master is requiring more of us than he has given us the power to perform. He tries to justify himself by laying the blame for his own sin of omission on God.

When the master says, "So you knew that I harvest where I have not sown and gather where I have not scattered seed?" (Matthew 25:26), he is speaking sarcastically. He is not agreeing with the accusation. Pointing out the hypocrisy of the servant's own words and actions, the master is essentially saying, "If you really think that I am that unfair, you should have put it in the bank to get interest, at the very least." When speaking elsewhere about the certainty that we will each give an account for the words we have spoken, Jesus says, "By your words you will be acquitted, and by your words you will be condemned" (Matthew 12:37).

Evangelist Oswald Chambers observes, "My vision of God is dependent upon the condition of my character. . . . I only see from the perspective of my own biases."[7] Just because the third servant claims that the master is stingy, hard, and aloof does not mean he is. Jesus is showing that the reasoning of the third servant is a smoke screen for inaction. When it comes time for settled accounts, we cannot wiggle our way out of the responsibility for our lives. You and I will be held responsible for doing our very best with what we have been assigned.

This is a story about generosity and opportunity compelled by love. Love alone holds people to the highest and best for their lives. People who don't love us neither give us anything nor expect anything from us.

NO SUCH THING AS NEGATIVE GOODNESS

The third servant is severely judged not for doing bad things but for doing nothing. He doesn't steal, embezzle, or defraud. It's critical to see that he is not judged because his investments failed; he is judged because he made no investment at all. He stood on the sidelines and did not jump in with both feet.

We can wrestle with this story. It would make more sense to us for him to be judged severely if he'd killed, lied, or cheated someone. But looking deeper, why did he do nothing? He did nothing because he believed the worst about the master. A wasted life is one of the greatest evils. Jesus used two words to describe this third servant: *wicked* and *lazy*. Although today we do not often link these words, Christians have historically taken laziness so seriously that it was listed as one of the seven deadly sins.

In our culture, some people say, "I can do whatever I want as long as I don't hurt anyone." But there is no such thing as negative goodness. Jesus' parable makes it clear that people around us can suffer not just when we actively hurt them but also when we withhold from them our very best efforts to steward well all the talents God has given us. A lifeguard may stand by and do nothing to help a drowning man, but that does not mean he has not hurt the man. There are sins of omission, not only sins of commission.

We do not like to admit our laziness. To be clear, God does call us to times of rest and Sabbath. Laziness is different. It's not rest; it's the temptation to do the minimum that meets the perceived standard rather than maximizing what we have been given. As part of my job, I often am involved in hiring staff members for our team. Whenever we ask a prospective team member what his or her greatest weakness is, it's always the same thing: "I work too hard and push myself too much." It's so cliché that we have now started telling people up front not to tell us that canned answer. When's the last time someone in an interview said, "My greatest weakness is that I like to sit on my couch eating ice cream and binge-watching Netflix"?

Jesus' story pairs the words *wicked* and *lazy*. Every single human being is capable of exuding these qualities. Spiritual maturity comes from maximizing what we have for the good of the Master's Kingdom. We can spend our whole lives waiting for the perfect moment to give our best rather than making the perfect moment now. The right time to do the right thing is right now. When we wait for some other future moment, it can lead to the sin of unrealized potential—the life that could have been, that God gave you the talent and opportunity to have but never happened. There is no neutral ground in this parable: Faithfulness provides more blessing; unfaithfulness results in loss of even one's initial blessings. By the very end of the parable, no one has the same amount they started out with. They either have more or none, but not the same.

Take a moment to assess what talents the Master has given you to manage well. Maybe you are like the first two servants, who went at once and got to work. If so, ask God to give you a reminder of how your decision to maximize what you have been given has made a difference for God's Kingdom. We often talk about grand plans, such as wanting to change the world. The truth is that most of us may never change the whole world, but we can change the world of those immediately around us. When that happens, it is a joy and a gift to be part of that. Our contribution really counts, matters, and makes a difference.

Or maybe you find yourself hesitant to jump in with both feet with your God-given talents to make a difference for God's Kingdom. How would the world around you be better if you were fully invested? Where in your life do you have a buried talent leading to unrealized potential? Your mind, your time, your talents, your attitude, your words, your prayers, your home—you can waste them or invest them. Your unique Kingdom contribution cannot be made by anyone else.

When we bury our talents, those around us suffer from their absence. The Master never asked how much we had to offer since he is the one who gave us the talents to begin with. Instead, he will want to know what we did with what we had. The world asks, "What does a person possess?" Christ asks, "How do they use it?"[8]

OVERCOMING THE FEAR OF FAILURE

The two faithful servants did not wait to get started. It is a smoke screen for us to wait for the perfect moment to use our talents for God's glory and the goodness of others. I am convinced that the thing that grieves the Master's heart is not a person who invests and fails but rather one who never invests at all. The third servant missed out on the joy of creating gain for the master's kingdom because he was controlled by the fear of failure. Often our greatest fear is failure but our greatest pain is regret. The ones who make it a habit of investing their talents will one day find success; those who make it a habit of hiding their talents guarantee that they never will.

A number of years ago, I felt compelled to use the church I

serve to help establish other churches in Los Angeles. The problem is that we had no guarantee of success, and I had never personally planted a church before. New congregations can be hard to start in urban settings. The living costs are high and so are the costs to rent any space. Parking spots are also an issue. I knew that it would not be easy. I feared that some of our church plants would fail.

In my own mind, I often debated all the reasons it would be better for someone else to try to do this. In fact, others already were, so I even thought maybe I should just cheer them on from the sideline. Slowly, we came to the realization that it was not a question of whether we were the best church to try to do this. We certainly were not. The only question became whether we were willing to try to use the talents we had to make a difference for the Master's Kingdom.

Just like the fear of failure can keep us from trying, the fear of regret can kick-start our courage to do something. Our leadership team concluded that at least we would not have to suffer the pain of regret of never trying. As Dr. Howard Hendricks once said to his students, "My fear is not that you would fail, but that you would succeed in doing the wrong thing."[9]

The truth is that some of our fears have come to pass. A couple of our initial church plants did not go well. That's putting it kindly. However, alongside those challenges, we had a few other plants that have not only done well but have grown beyond our wildest hopes.

Lives are being affected. Justice is being done. People who were once far from God are coming to know Christ. Leaders are being developed. Faith is rising. We are not guaranteed first-time success. However, if we make it a habit to keep investing our talents, we will eventually find success as God flourishes our efforts while we learn and grow. Again, from Hendricks, "There's no such thing as faith apart from risk-taking. Creativity takes risk. The people who are most secure in Jesus Christ shouldn't be scared to try new things."[10]

GENEROUS GIFTS, SETTLED ACCOUNTS, AND LAVISH REWARDS

By the end of the story, we see that the one who started out in the parable being so generous in his gift giving is now lavish in his rewards given. Notice that the master does not say, "Well done, good and faithful servant. Now float on fluffy clouds, play a harp, and sing the same song over and over again for a billion years." Instead, he says, "Well done, good and faithful servant. Let's celebrate! And I'll give you even more." The master's abundance is shared (see Matthew 25:29) as well as his joy (see verses 21 and 23). Likewise, it is the faithfulness with what God has given you today that prepares you to be commended with even more in the future.

In Revelation, Jesus says that all who are faithful to the end will reign and rule with him forever (see Revelation 2:26; 3:21). No more effects of sin. No more frustration as we know it. Part of heaven's reward will be seeing the full potential of your humanity realized—seeing the impact of being "both feet" kind of people.

Luke's version of this parable says that the master will put the faithful servants in charge of cities. If you are investing your God-given talents to the best of your abilities to make your unique contribution to God's Kingdom, well done! If not, what are you waiting for?

Do not wait a moment longer. The right time to do the right thing is right now.

CHAPTER 6

THE SUREFIRE WAY TO ENSURE YOUR UNHAPPINESS

The Story of the Vineyard Workers

Envy is the art of counting the other fellow's blessings instead of your own.

HAROLD COFFIN

Jesus Christ did not say, "Go into all the world and
tell the world that it is quite right."

C. S. LEWIS

IT CAN BE A PAINFUL THING not to keep your eyes on your own path.

In college, I played rugby, which is a sport that involves a lot of running. To keep our conditioning runs interesting, our team decided to jog through the historic district of the town. As we were running on the sidewalk, something happened on the street. It might have been a hot rod that revved its engine, but to this day I cannot remember exactly what it was. But I do recall what happened next.

As I was running, I took a quick glimpse to the side to see what was happening on the street. When I did that, somehow, magically, a parking meter sprouted up right in front of me! It was one of those moments in life when you know something bad is about to happen but you are powerless to stop it. So with shoppers watching and my merciless teammates alongside, I ran full speed into a parking meter. Apparently, my momentary look to my right took me two steps to my right, which was two steps too many.

My collision with the parking meter knocked all the wind out of me. I dropped to the sidewalk, doubled over and trying to regain my breath, to which one of my teammates dryly shared, "Well, I guess that's what you get when you don't keep your eyes on your own path." Gee, thanks.

Sideways glances do not happen just when we are running; they can happen when we are living our everyday lives. They happen in the form of comparing ourselves, our lives, and our opportunities with others. Instead of knocking the wind out of us, such comparisons knock the gratitude out of us. Comparison is the thief of joy.[1] Jesus once told a story about that very thing and how destructive it is for our eyes to drift from our own paths.

A STORY OF COMPARISON AND ENVY

Jesus tells the story this way:

> The kingdom of heaven is like a landowner who went out early in the morning to hire workers for his vineyard. He agreed to pay them a denarius for the day and sent them into his vineyard.
>
> About nine in the morning he went out and saw others standing in the marketplace doing nothing. He told them, "You also go and work in my vineyard, and I will pay you whatever is right." So they went.

He went out again about noon and about three in the afternoon and did the same thing. About five in the afternoon he went out and found still others standing around. He asked them, "Why have you been standing here all day long doing nothing?"

"Because no one has hired us," they answered.

He said to them, "You also go and work in my vineyard."

When evening came, the owner of the vineyard said to his foreman, "Call the workers and pay them their wages, beginning with the last ones hired and going on to the first."

The workers who were hired about five in the afternoon came and each received a denarius. So when those came who were hired first, they expected to receive more. But each one of them also received a denarius. When they received it, they began to grumble against the landowner. "These who were hired last worked only one hour," they said "and you have made them equal to us who have borne the burden of the work and the heat of the day."

But he answered one of them, "I am not being unfair to you, friend. Didn't you agree to work for a denarius? Take your pay and go. I want to give the one who was hired last the same as I gave you. Don't I have the right to do what I want with my own money? Or are you envious because I am generous?"

So the last will be first, and the first will be last.

MATTHEW 20:1-16

Jesus throws this story alongside our hearts to confront one of life's most common occurrences. In the parable, the owner starts at 6 a.m. but then returns throughout the day: 9 a.m., noon, 3 p.m. Each time he sends out more workers to the field. The last group is sent out at 5 p.m. It is the eleventh hour of a twelve-hour workday.

At this point in the story, everybody is satisfied, at least partially. With some of them having started the day with no guarantee of anything, they all now will at least receive something. They are all better off than when the story began. These were day laborers who lived off the work they did that day. No work would mean no food that night for them or their families. Everyone at this point is relieved and grateful not to be headed home empty handed to a houseful of hungry children.

Because the first workers are paid last, they have a chance to take a peek at what the other groups of workers are being paid. They are delighted when they see the groups ahead of them graciously being paid a full day's wage even though those workers did not work a full twelve-hour day. They are delighted not for the generosity given to the other workers but because they now presume they will be paid more. But when they get to the table, they are given one full day's wage like all the rest before them.

Had those who worked the longest been paid first, they would have left content, satisfied, and happy. They got what they'd agreed to at the beginning of the day: a fair day's pay for a fair day's work. The landowner was true to his word and just in his payment. But now they are furious. They are furious with what would have satisfied them (and what they originally agreed to at the start of the day). That's what comparison does: It provokes us to overestimate what we need and underestimate what we already have. One of the great tests of our hearts is to decide to be genuinely happy for others when things are going well for them without wondering why the same is not now happening for us.

THEIR BEST MOMENTS VERSUS OUR MUNDANE ONES

The rise of social media has created more opportunities than ever before to take comparing looks into our friends' lives. I am not anti-technology, but now it's no longer just comparison; now it is comparison with the edited, filtered, and packaged pictures that give us only a selected portal into the lives of our friends. We see their best moments and measure them against our mundane ones. It's the same with what we let them see in our lives through our posts. Author Shauna Niequist nails the challenge of social media when it comes to comparison:

> It's very, very easy to tell partial truths—to show the fabulous meal but not the mess to clean up afterward. To display the smiling couple-shot, but not the fight you had three days ago. To offer up the sparkly milestones but not the spiraling meltdowns.[2]

Of course, we do not need social media to fall prey to the trap of comparison. Yet in today's world, those who would be waiting to be paid last would not even have to go looking for the comparison. The workers on the receiving end of the extravagant act of generosity of the landowner would have posted about it on their Instagram story within the hour. With social media, sometimes the envy-creating comparison comes looking for you.

Those who worked the longest made their case for their perceived injustice. Admittedly, from their vantage point, this does seem patently unfair. That's the thing about grace: It is always unfair. It never seems more unfair and unjust than when you think you are not the recipient of it and others are. The owner responds, "Listen, there has been no injustice here. I paid you exactly what I agreed to pay you at 6 a.m." Then the owner brings us to the pivotal questions of the whole story: "Am I not free to do with my abundance what I want? Or will you be embittered because I am generous?" When you ignore God's goodness to you, you tend to resent his goodness to others.

Theologian D. A. Carson rightly sees the danger of constant comparison and complaint to the health of our souls:

> Persistent negativism is spiritually perilous. The person who makes it his life's ambition to discover all the things that are wrong . . . is exposing himself to spiritual destruction. Thankfulness to God both for good things and for his sovereign protection and purpose even in bad things will be the first virtue to go. It will be quickly followed by humility, as the critic, deeply knowledgeable about faults and fallacies (especially those of others!), comes to feel superior to those whom he criticizes. Spiritual one-upmanship is not a Christian virtue. Sustained negativism is highly calorific nourishment for pride.[3]

YOU WILL FIND WHAT YOU ARE LOOKING FOR

This parable affirms the sovereign grace of God while it rejects presuming grace or comparing it. Grace is always amazing grace. Grace that can be calculated and expected is no longer grace. Comparison often leads to envy, which has a boomerang effect on our souls. As novelist Aleksandr Solzhenitsyn saw, "Our envy of others devours us most of all."[4] Here is a surefire way to guarantee your unhappiness: spend a lot of time comparing your life to others'.

Whether we look for reasons to be grateful or to complain, we will find what we are looking for. It's a bit like the difference between a vulture and a hummingbird. The vulture starts out the day looking for death. Because that is what it has set its heart to look for, sure enough, it will find it. The hummingbird starts out the day looking for the sweet nectar in life. Because that is what it has set its heart to look for, sure enough, it will find it. Even in our brightest hour, there is something bad we can gripe about. Even in our darkest hour, there is something good we can see.

A while back I was at Hume Lake Christian Camp for an all-staff retreat we had planned. It's a gorgeous camp with a lake nestled among the pine trees immediately adjacent to Kings Canyon National Park in the Sierra Nevada Mountains of California. The camp looks like a postcard for serene beauty. I had arrived an hour early to simply verify that everything was prepared for our soon-to-arrive staff.

During the check-in process, one of the people helping me told me how envious he was that I got to live in Los Angeles. He commented on all the amenities, the things to do, the energy and excitement of the city. And yes, much of what he said is absolutely true. Los Angeles has world-class amenities, food, activities, beaches, and more. But I softly chuckled when he said this.

He asked, "Why the laugh?"

I responded, "Oh, I was just thinking about how great you have it to live in the midst of all this quiet and beauty in the mountains, with the lake and the nearby waterfalls. Plus, you never have to sit in traffic here." We tend to see what we are looking for.

WHEN LIFE IS UNFAIR IN OUR FAVOR

Sometimes life's unfairness falls in our favor. When we are the beneficiaries of unmerited favor, most of us don't complain. The poker player dealt four aces does not ask for a re-deal because of the injustice done to other players by his being dealt such a fabulous hand. We seem acutely attuned to detect anytime life is unfair against us. However, when the roles are reversed, our sensitivities often fail us.

Most times, there is no win in comparison. It usually leads to either pride or discouragement. If you compare yourself with others who are not doing as well, your heart is tempted to puff up in pride: "Well, I am getting ahead. I am doing better than that person. I must *be* better than that person." Conversely, if you compare yourself with others who are doing better than you, your heart is tempted to feel discouraged: "What's wrong with me? Why can't I have their lives?"

In this chapter's parable, when the owner chooses the first workers at the start of the day, there is nothing of merit in the selection. Jesus' story gives us no indication that those chosen had better grape-picking résumés, grape-picking interviewing skills, grape-picking educations, or grape-picking work ethics. Yes, they have a full day of work ahead of them, but their initial selection over the others is still an act of grace.

Those of us born in the United States or some other wealthy country don't say, "You know, it's not fair that I was born in this situation. I'm going to renounce my citizenship and move to a more impoverished country with less opportunity for me."

Recently, I was with a pastor who was telling me all the challenges he faces leading the congregation he serves. I felt great sympathy for him, but you know what I did not do? I did not go home that night and pray, "Lord, why have you been so unjust in my favor to allow me to serve the church I serve? Maybe I should see if the other pastor and I can switch roles. He can take my role, and I'll take on his divided, frustrated, and wounded congregation." Before we zero in on how life has been unfair to us, we do well to pause and remember how it has been unfair in our favor, too.

THE DOWN-TO-EARTH ANTIDOTE TO COMPARISON

What if each person in the parable compared their situation with only their own situation at the beginning of the story? Instead of thinking, *What did they get?* how about if we thought, *What do I have that I didn't have when my story started?* In other words, what if we started with the idea that even being born at all is a bonanza, a gift, an act of generosity from the Creator? Because it is.

Here are the stark facts: None of us willed, worked, or earned ourselves into existence. Like the workers who were totally at the mercy of the landowner for any sort of employment, each of us did not set into motion the process that God used to create us. Commenting on this parable, John Claypool discerns,

> The beginning point of this parable is *grace*, not entitlement, and the same is true of life as well. Birth is windfall, and life is gift. We were called out of nothing into being in an astonishing act of generosity for which we can claim no right. Once that gift becomes our central focus, it changes forever how we interpret things.[5]

In English, our phrase *to thank* comes from the same root for our phrase *to think*. How you think determines who you thank. God wanted to give you the gift of life. You did not do anything to deserve it; it's just part of his generosity. The more you think about that, the more you will begin to "thank" about that.

I once read the true story of a family who excitedly awaited the birth of their fifth child.[6] Everyone gathered at the hospital on the night of her arrival. She was perfect, but for some reason she had no arms or legs. The doctors had no explanation of why this had happened. The parents made a decision to take this daughter as she was born and count her life as a grace. They gave her every opportunity to lead a normal life, under the circumstances.

She lived to be twenty-one and by all accounts was a delightful, hopeful, joyful, and thankful woman. She had a brilliant mind, a witty sense of humor, and a remarkable capacity for friendship with people rich, poor, young, old, and of various ethnicities—all in spite of the fact that she never once was able to do many of the everyday things that most of us take for granted.

She was once asked, "What keeps you from blowing up in anger at whatever kind of God would have let you be born into this world in this condition? How do you keep from becoming a volcano of resentment?"

The young woman looked her inquirer straight in the eyes and responded,

I realize that compared to what most people have, what I have does not seem like much. But listen, I have been able to see and hear. I've been able to smell and taste and feel. I have been exposed to some of the world's great literature and heard some of the finest music ever composed. I've had some of the most wonderful friendships that anyone could ever have. I know what I have does not seem like much when compared to what other people have, but when compared to never getting to be at all, I would not have missed being born for anything!"[7]

When you choose gratitude over comparison, its impact on your life is far reaching. Studies have shown that gratitude makes us more social, leading to better friendships and even a healthier marriage. Emotionally, gratitude makes us more resilient and more relaxed in life. At work, we become better at making decisions and increase our productivity. Benefits for health include improved sleep, increased energy, and becoming sick less often.[8] If gratitude came in a pill form, it would be considered a wonder drug![9] Just like all the workers in the parable ended the day with more than they had started their story with, the same is true of us in our stories.

EFFORT VERSUS EARNING

Jesus tells the worker parable in response to Peter mentioning that he and the other disciples had left everything to follow Jesus. "What then will there be for us?" Peter asks (Matthew 19:27). Jesus answered,

> Truly I tell you, at the renewal of all things, when the Son of Man sits on his glorious throne, you who have followed me will also sit on twelve thrones, judging the twelve tribes of Israel. And everyone who has left houses or brothers or sisters or father or mother or wife or children or fields

for my sake will receive a hundred times as much and will inherit eternal life. But many who are first will be last, and many who are last will be first.

MATTHEW 19:28-30

Jesus later states a version of that last phrase, with only the parable sandwiched in between.

Sacrifice in following Jesus is not about what we gain as a result; rather, it is in response to what has already been given to us. As philosopher and author Dallas Willard writes, "Grace is not opposed to effort, it is opposed to earning. Earning is an attitude. Effort is an action."[10] It's not that gain does not come, because Jesus is clear that it does. Yes, Peter and the others had left much to follow Jesus, but Jesus had left everything to redeem Peter and the other followers of Jesus. God's saving grace has nothing to do with the amount of time we have served him. The dying thief on the cross who placed his faith in Jesus is welcomed into the Kingdom no less than the person who has served Christ for many years. Just because God's generosity is available to the genuine latecomers should not diminish the astonishing fact that it is available to any of us, including those who arrived at the vineyard early in the day.

In the workers who were bitter in their comparison, Jesus paints us a picture of what not to become. But in his story, he also illustrates what is possible for us to become. The workers were not the only ones who were looking around at others. The owner also had the habit of taking a look around. Only he was not looking around with eyes of comparison; he was looking with eyes of compassion.

Earlier, I said that most times there is no win in comparison. The reason for *most times* is that God can certainly redeem even our wandering eyes of comparison. Such redemption happens when we compare our lives with others who are less fortunate than we are, allowing the assessment to create compassion, solidarity, and advocacy for the poor. Redemption also happens each time a person who has been lost is saved and a longtime follower of Jesus celebrates rather than whining about why the new believer is being offered the same benefits for such a late entry into the vineyard of God's Kingdom.

The owner realized that all the workers had families to feed and needed a whole day's wage. In deciding to pay them as he did, the owner is not calculating the value of the service that he had received from them; he is thinking about what is best for them. It is his generosity, his grace, that is the genesis of his actions. When we see that happen in another person's life, we can either moan about it or be thankful that such a generous God comes to meet us in our lives too.

That day I went for a run with my rugby team, I got the wind knocked out of me because I was focused on the wrong thing. So let me ask you this: In what areas of your life do you need to keep your eyes focused on your own path? In what ways are you letting sideways glimpses of comparison knock the wind of gratitude and contentment out of you? Jesus tells this story so we would keep our stories focused on the joy and gratitude we were created to know by removing the comparisons that we were never created to make.

CHAPTER 7

DOING FIRST
WHAT MATTERS MOST

The Story of the Ten Bridesmaids

> It is not enough to be busy; so are the ants. The question is:
> What are we busy about?
>
> **HENRY DAVID THOREAU**

> I knew that if I failed, I wouldn't regret that. But I knew the one thing
> I might regret is not ever having tried.
>
> **JEFF BEZOS**

WHAT'S YOUR BIGGEST REGRET IN LIFE?

Students from a local university set up a chalkboard on a sidewalk near Lieutenant Joseph Petrosino Square in New York City for one day. At the top of the board was written a simple statement: "Write your biggest regret." They provided a supply of colored chalk. The chalkboard grabbed the attention of many of the people walking by, and slowly but surely, it filled to overflowing with written regrets that were poignant and thought provoking.

Burning bridges. Not speaking up. Not being a good husband. Not spending enough time with family. Not saying "I love you." Never applying to medical school. Not making the most of every day. Not being a better friend. Not leaving one's comfort zone.

As the board filled up with so many different phrases, the

students noticed that almost all of the phrases of regret had one thing in common: Nearly all of them involved the word *not*. They were about words not spoken, dreams not pursued, and relationships not repaired.[1]

Jesus tells a parable that is about the two saddest words in the English language: *too late*. Like college students who are in the midst of a semester-long class, everyone knows that the final exam is coming, so it is wise to be prepared for it. On the day of the exam, for unprepared students, it is too late. They will regret it, but they will not be able to turn back the hands of time. This is true about life. It's also probably one of the most denied and avoided truths. At one point, Jesus tells four stories in a row that serve the purpose to bold, underline, and italicize the fact that one day there will be a final exam, but on that day, it will be too late to prepare (see Matthew 24:45–25:46). However, Jesus is telling us these stories because it is not too late now. He is like a professor who says in advance to pay attention to this because it will be on the final exam. When a professor says that, we have a choice: Either we can ignore him, or we can receive it as an act of grace from someone who wants his students to be prepared to graduate.

A STORY OF REGRET

Jesus begins the story,

> The Kingdom of Heaven will be like ten bridesmaids who
> took their lamps and went to meet the bridegroom. Five
> of them were foolish, and five were wise. The five who
> were foolish didn't take enough olive oil for their lamps,

but the other five were wise enough to take along extra oil. When the bridegroom was delayed, they all became drowsy and fell asleep.

At midnight they were roused by the shout, "Look, the bridegroom is coming! Come out and meet him!"

All the bridesmaids got up and prepared their lamps. Then the five foolish ones asked the others, "Please give us some of your oil because our lamps are going out."

But the others replied, "We don't have enough for all of us. Go to a shop and buy some for yourselves."

But while they were gone to buy oil, the bridegroom came. Then those who were ready went in with him to the marriage feast, and the door was locked. Later, when the other five bridesmaids returned, they stood outside, calling, "Lord! Lord! Open the door for us!"

But he called back, "Believe me, I don't know you!"

So you, too, must keep watch! For you do not know the day or hour of my return.

MATTHEW 25:1-13 (NLT)

WE ARE NOT JUST RUNNING IN CIRCLES

First-century people knew how to party. A wedding celebration went on for days, not just hours. Near the end of the multiday celebration, the groom would come to the home of the bride and escort her to the final ceremony.

It was this act that was the formal recognition of their union, which was always accompanied by even more celebration. Before a groom would come, a friend of his would precede him to say,

"Look! Here is the groom! Come out to meet him as he arrives." In American culture, we often say, "Here comes the bride!" but in those days, it was rather, "Here comes the groom!"

In this story, the groom is delayed, although the people are not told for how long. He will come. The groom is a picture of the Messiah, who is Jesus. What Jesus is saying is that he is going to return on the appointed day. He will come for his bride, and all the wrongs on earth will be set right. God's intended order will be restored in completion.

Jesus is throwing this story alongside us to awaken us to the fact that life is not some random cycle of events. Just because you feel as though you are running around in circles does not mean you are. There is an old Bill Murray movie called *Groundhog Day*, which has the plot that every day is just a repeat of the previous one. But this is not like that. Just as your life had a beginning, it will also have an end. Each of our choices matter, and ultimately we will be judged. Jesus tells us this so we understand that we are to live in the light of this truth: The Groom is coming back, so be prepared and have oil in your lamps.

It is helpful to think of the lamps as our lives, and the oil as the deeds and attitudes of our hearts that fill our lives. This is not simply conjecture. In his most famous message, called the Sermon on the Mount, Jesus told those gathered, "You are the light of the world—like a city on a hilltop that cannot be hidden. No one lights a lamp and puts it under a basket. Instead, a lamp is placed on a stand, where it gives light to everyone in the house. In the same way, let your good deeds shine out for all to see, so that everyone will praise your heavenly Father" (Matthew 5:14-16, NLT).

DOING FIRST WHAT MATTERS MOST

The bridesmaids are given only one task: to make sure their lamps are ready for the celebration. Five of the bridesmaids are not ready. There is no oil in their lamps left to burn. They ask to borrow oil from the five wise bridesmaids, but they say no. The answer seems so selfish. Why won't they lend oil to the five foolish bridesmaids?

The point is this: Some things cannot be borrowed.

A relationship with God cannot be borrowed. It must be done yourself. Character cannot be borrowed. Deeds done out of love and obedience to Jesus cannot be borrowed. Faith cannot be borrowed. A life cannot be borrowed. Jesus is driving home this truth that we all try to evade: Each of us alone is responsible before God for what we decide to do with our one and only life.

I have no control over my genes. I have no control over what parents I was born to. However, I do have control over my choices: my ability to choose between good and evil, to choose love or hate, and to choose the path of faith or unfaithfulness. I have it within my power to choose to act rather than be passive. So many of the people on that New York sidewalk wrote about regrets of passivity or regrets based on fear. It was about what they did not do. Each of us make hundreds of decisions that knit together the fabric of our souls. We cannot borrow our souls from anyone else.

Not only can some things not be borrowed, but there is an even deeper, more sobering truth contained in this soul story: It is possible to wait too long. We must do first what matters most, yet sometimes we think we have forever, so we delay doing what matters most. We can see this in life and even in art.

In Berlin's Old National Gallery is the fascinating painting by German painter Adolph Menzel entitled *Frederick the Great*

Addresses His Generals before the Battle of Leuthen in 1757. It's only partially finished. What is interesting is what is left out. He intended to show the king, Frederick the Great, speaking with some of his generals. Menzel painted the background and generals but left the king until last. He put in an outline of Frederick in charcoal but died prior to finishing it. Menzel failed to put into the picture the one person who mattered most.

Having left the king until last, he didn't include him in the picture at all. Menzel assumed he had forever to do first what mattered most, but he didn't. And neither do we. C. S. Lewis was right when he observed, "Put first things first and we get second things thrown in: put second things first and we lose *both* first and second things."[2]

Jesus' parable about the bridesmaids is about the primacy of the most important thing in life. It's not too late now, but one day it will be. The bridesmaids cannot borrow oil, so they run out trying to purchase some. But keep in mind, it is midnight. It is too late. The stores are closed. While the groom was delayed, they lacked a sense of priority and urgency. They thought they had all the time in the world. They were distracted when they should have been focused. Sliding into believing that everything mattered equally, they did not do the one thing that mattered most: have oil ready for their lamps.

Life is weird that way. Have you ever noticed that sometimes the days feel long but the years feel short? The same person can say, "I had the longest day today," and then declare, "I cannot believe it is summer again. This year is flying by!" Jesus was clear that we have a set amount of time to do the good works that God has prepared for us to do.

On a different occasion, Jesus said it this way: "We must

quickly carry out the tasks assigned us by the one who sent us. The night is coming, and then no one can work. But while I am here in the world, I am the light of the world" (John 9:4-5, NLT). There is an urgency to do the tasks God has assigned for each of us to do. We must be seized with the urgency of this moment, this day, this time, because it will not last forever. Jesus tells this story so that we will not be forced to suffer the pain of regret.

All the bridesmaids had the opportunity, but for five of them, it is now too late for them. It leads to these soul-haunting words: "If only . . ." The story is not about trying to figure out when the groom is coming in order to cram for the final exam. God has no interest in end-times predictions and calculations (see Mark 13:32-33). God is interested in one thing: transformed hearts that create an overflow of good works done from the heart. That is all that matters, and five of the bridesmaids are unprepared.

IS GOD'S GRACE INFINITE?

So the big question is this: How do people fail at living for the one thing they should be living for? Notice that Jesus does not call these people evil or wicked; he calls them foolish. If they were asked why they did not get oil, they would most likely say what kids everywhere say when asked why they did something foolish: "I don't know." They just drift, and life slips through their fingers while they're consumed with secondary issues. The tyranny of the urgent becomes the foundation of regret.

Complacency can strike the soul of every human being. We do not want to say that we gave our lives away to lesser pursuits. We do not want to say, "I let life drift away." The parable of the ten bridesmaids makes it clear: The Kingdom is a prepared place for prepared people, and some things cannot be borrowed.

Theologian and bishop Will Willimon once recounted an experience from his life:

> Early in my ministry, I served a little church in rural Georgia. One Saturday we went to a funeral in a little country church not of my denomination. I grew up in a big downtown church. I had never been to a funeral like this one. The casket was open, and the funeral consisted of a sermon by their preacher.
>
> The preacher pounded on the pulpit and looked over at the casket. He said, "It's too late for Joe. He might have wanted to get his life together. He might have wanted to spend more time with his family. He might have wanted to do that, but he's dead now. It is too late for him, but it is not too late for you."[3]

Willimon was so angry at that preacher. On the way home, he told his wife, "Have you ever seen anything as manipulative and insensitive to that poor family? I found it disgusting."

She said, "I've never heard anything like that. It was manipulative. It was disgusting. It was insensitive. Worst of all, it was also true."[4]

Now, you might be wondering where the grace of God is in all this. Remember that Jesus is telling us, through the bridesmaid parable, that one day it will be too late, but *it is not too late now*. That is an act of mercy and grace. It's important to see that it may not be too late now but that one day it will be. Theologian and author R. C. Sproul cautions us against mistaking God's available grace for infinite grace. He says,

> God's grace is not infinite. God is infinite, and God is gracious. We experience the grace of an infinite God, but grace is not infinite. God sets limits to His patience and forbearance. He warns us over and over again that someday the ax will fall and His judgment will be poured out.[5]

Faith in Christ not only saves us *from* something, it also saves us *for* something. It saves us so we can become the people God has always dreamed of us becoming: saved by grace so we will be empowered to live out the good deeds he has prepared for each of us to do before the world began (see Ephesians 2:8-10). In telling us his parable, Jesus is like a professor telling us in advance what will be on the final exam. One day it will be too late, but today it is not too late.

THE POWER FOR A NEW FUTURE NOW

Remember those students who set up the chalkboard on the sidewalk in New York City and had people write down their regrets? The students eventually gave these same people an eraser and wrote "Clean Slate" at the top of the chalkboard, although the point is not that past regrets can simply be erased. Few people are naive enough to believe that from their experience of life. Regrets can be forgiven but not just erased. The point was that today is a new beginning. We cannot go backward, but we can go forward from this moment with the wisdom learned from our past regrets.

Our pasts may not be different, but our futures can be empowered by the reflections of how not to repeat our regrets. As one young woman stared at the blank chalkboard with a clean slate, she had tears in her eyes as she said, "It's hopeful. It means there's possibility."[6]

What about you? Are there regrets that you feel compelled to amend? You cannot rewind time, but you can do this day differently. It could be that there is a person you need to call and ask forgiveness from. It might be that today is the day you choose with God's help to start a legacy of generosity. Maybe God has put a person or two in your relational world who needs to hear the gospel of Jesus.

It could be that you see that God is asking you to speak up and act for biblical justice for those who are marginalized in our world, including the poor, the foreigner, and the outcast. Clean slates are worthless if our passivity just fills them anew with a repeat of fresh regrets of what we did not do. Or maybe, if you are not a Christian, you sense the urgency to figure out what is genuinely true about Jesus. Who is he, and why does it matter?

Today you have a new day. What will you do with it?

May you keep putting oil in your lamps with the urgency that knows that it is grace that compels you to light up a dark world with the good deeds God has prepared for you to do. It is not too late now, but one day it will be. Jesus does not want you to squander the great gift of your life on always waiting until tomorrow to do what you can do today. In other words, if your life is a painting about the king, make certain you put him in first and everything else second.

CHAPTER 8

THE JOY OF SPENDING SOMEONE ELSE'S MONEY

The Story of the Dishonest Manager

He is no fool who gives what he cannot keep
to gain that which he cannot lose.

JIM ELLIOT

No one has ever become poor by giving.

ANNE FRANK

A MAN HAPPENED TO BE WALKING along the streets of the city, when suddenly an armed robber approached him and ordered, "Your money or your life!" There was a long pause, and the man did nothing. He just stood there.

The thief impatiently asked, "Well?"

The man replied, "Don't rush me—I'm thinking about it."

Money certainly plays a role in all our lives, and sometimes it can become too important of a role. Some people think that money is not a very spiritual topic, but they would be wrong. For example, the Bible has five hundred verses on prayer, less than five hundred on faith, but more than two thousand on money and possessions.[1] We can begin to see Jesus as a gadfly, provoking us with his stories. In fact, the parable we are about to look at left those who loved money ridiculing Jesus (see Luke 16:14).

This parable is known as the story of the dishonest manager. It is one of Jesus' most unusual stories:

There was a rich man whose manager was accused of wasting his possessions. So he called him in and asked him, "What is this I hear about you? Give an account of your management, because you cannot be manager any longer."

The manager said to himself, "What shall I do now? My master is taking away my job. I'm not strong enough to dig, and I'm ashamed to beg—I know what I'll do so that, when I lose my job here, people will welcome me into their houses."

So he called in each one of his master's debtors. He asked the first, "How much do you owe my master?"

"Nine hundred gallons of olive oil," he replied.

The manager told him, "Take your bill, sit down quickly, and make it four hundred and fifty."

Then he asked the second, "And how much do you owe?"

"A thousand bushels of wheat," he replied.

He told him, "Take your bill and make it eight hundred."

The master commended the dishonest manager because he had acted shrewdly. For the people of this world are more shrewd in dealing with their own kind than are the people of the light. I tell you, use worldly wealth to gain friends for yourselves, so that when it is gone, you will be welcomed into eternal dwellings.

LUKE 16:1-9

THE FIRST SEVEN WORDS

The first seven words of this story might be the most critical for us: "There was a rich man whose manager . . ." So then here's the question: Do we see ourselves as the owner or the manager? Scripture tells us explicitly, "You may say to yourself, 'My power and the strength of my hands have produced this wealth for me.' But remember the LORD your God, for it is he who gives you the ability to produce wealth" (Deuteronomy 8:17-18). This parable begins with a foundational truth for us to integrate into our lives: We are not the owner; we only *know* the owner. We are the manager.

When I was in high school, I used to think that what I had was *my* money. I worked for it. It's not as if someone was just giving it away on the street corner. It seemed pretty clear to me that my income required me to spend my power, my effort, and my toil. Then one day a mentor in the faith gently reminded me that the best of my efforts, talents, opportunities, and abilities come from God. If he wanted to, he could take any of it or all of it away from me. The mentor observed that I am not entitled to any of it.

It was shocking to hear. It was also true.

It's one thing to know that we are the manager in Jesus' story; it's quite another to live that way in our everyday lives. Jesus is telling this parable to his disciples. If we genuinely believe that God is the rich man and we are the managers, then that means something for our discipleship. It means that generosity becomes the new natural for us. Conversely, if you think that you are the genuine owner of all you have, you will constantly struggle to understand how generosity can be a joy.

SELF-TALK ON MONEY MANAGEMENT

Jesus continues the story with charges brought that the manager is wasting the owner's possessions. The owner calls the manager in for the final accounting because his time as the manager is over. We won't be the manager in our stories forever either. The manager is clearly guilty as charged. He makes no attempt to explain or defend himself to the owner. Instead, he begins to do what all sane and rational people do: He talks to himself.

Self-talk is something we all do. But it's important to think about what you talk to yourself about. To live differently, you have to think differently. To think differently, you have to monitor your thoughts—your self-talk. God's Word tells us that we are "transformed by the renewing of [our] mind" (Romans 12:2).

Notice here that the man's upcoming actions result directly from his thinking. The same is true for us. Through his self-talk, he correctly assesses the lay of the landscape. He realizes that he is too weak for manual labor and too proud to beg. He is insightful enough to know that this requires decisive action.

In the story, the master has apparently lent out his land to tenants, who have agreed to pay him a fixed return in grain or oil. In response to his imminent crisis, the steward calls in the rich man's debtors and summarily reduces the debt of each. These are not small household quantities. The debtors are large-scale business associates, not ordinary people with average economic levels. In Jesus' day, the validity of the contract is guaranteed by being written in the handwriting of the debtor, with the document kept in the possession of the manager. The manager acts now with an eye to his quickly coming future needs of shelter and food when his job is done.

THE CURIOUS TWIST IN THE PARABLE

There is a strange turn in this parable: The dishonest manager is actually commended! That seems weird, at first. But notice that he is not commended for his initial mismanagement of the owner's resources. Instead, he is commended for acting shrewdly when he knew his time was limited. He is considered shrewd rather than simply cheating, because his actions cast an aura of goodness and generosity on the rich man while simultaneously providing for his own future by ingratiating himself with the rich man's debtors.

Because he has done this favor for them, he is providing for his future well-being, as he is about to lose both his job and shelter (managers often lived on the owner's property). The rich man then is not praising him for his dishonesty; he is praising him for the great foresight to anticipate what he will need after his dismissal and for using his current situation to make the most of his future one.

After concluding the parable, Jesus goes on to say,

> If you have not been trustworthy in handling worldly wealth, who will trust you with true riches? And if you have not been trustworthy with someone else's property, who will give you property of your own?
>
> No one can serve two masters. Either you will hate the one and love the other, or you will be devoted to the one and despise the other. You cannot serve both God and money.
>
> LUKE 16:11-13

Any financial planner will tell you that you have to start with the end in mind. You have to start from knowing what you want your future to look like. Most of the time, this refers to retirement, but Jesus' parable is saying that we need to extend that timeline a bit further: into eternity.

Repeatedly in his parables addressing money, Jesus taught his disciples to use their money to wisely invest in Kingdom purposes. It's true in this parable. It's true in the parable of Lazarus and the rich man (see Luke 16:19-31). It's also true in the parable of the rich fool (see Luke 12:16-21).

There is no waffling. We cannot serve both God and money. Either we will choose to submit the money we have to God, or it will become our god. Money makes a great tool, but it is a terrible master.

Jesus' parable is saying that we are the manager now but will not be forever. Time is short. Decisive action now with what we cannot keep will in some way make a difference in our futures. The road to who we are becoming in the eternal future begins now. The cunning manager saw this. Do we? That is what Jesus' parable is asking. It reminds me of Jim Elliot's famous quote, "He is no fool who gives what he cannot keep to gain that which he cannot lose."

BECOMING A SHREWD, FAITHFUL, AND GENEROUS MANAGER

A discerning manager has an urgency to act now, not later.

When I was younger and first heard this parable, I began to pay attention to my inner self-talk. What I realized was that I was constantly erecting mental barriers to obedience. I told myself that I would be more generous later: once I had paid off the car loans, once I paid off more student loans, and so on. Have you ever noticed there is always a reason to delay generosity?

In his words immediately following this parable, Jesus rejects that line of self-talk as being in denial. We will not be different when we have more; we will be different when we decide to change with God's help. Jesus calls it faithfulness. He says, "Whoever can be trusted with very little can also be trusted with much, and whoever is dishonest with very little will also be dishonest with much" (Luke 16:10). Why is that the case? Because generosity is never about how much money we have; it's about how much of our hearts God has. Jesus' comments coupled with this parable make it clear that God is looking for wise and faithful managers.

This manager was not just shrewd; he was also generous to the others in the story. At first we may think, *Well, how can he be considered generous when it was not even his money? It was the rich man's money!* Exactly. That's our situation too. It's the rich man's money. We just get to use it to be generous with others. There's nothing like the joy of spending someone else's money!

It's easy to see that Jesus intends for us to identify with the manager in the story. It's often more challenging to act like-wise in our own stories. Case in point: tithing. The word *tithe* means "tenth."[2] The Bible repeatedly mentions God's command to give 10 percent of our income back to him in worship (see Malachi 3:8-12). Jesus also affirms tithing while also challenging us not to neglect the weightier issues of justice, mercy, and faithfulness (see Matthew 23:23). Tithing is not the end of generosity but rather the beginning of it. Genuine generosity can go much further (see Luke 19:8; Acts 4:32).

Over the years, I have used a recurring illustration in our church's weekend services when I teach on the joy of generosity. I ask for a volunteer to come up front with me. In my hand, I hold 111 dollars. I asked them whose money it is. They usually say it is mine. One time a biblically savvy volunteer said it's God's money and that I was only holding it for the moment! Either answer works, as long as they see it is not theirs.

Giving them the 111 dollars, I then ask them to give me back 10 percent (eleven dollars, using rounded figures). Every single person I have ever done this with has given me back the eleven dollars. I then ask them whether it was hard or easy to do. Of course, they say it was easy. Why was it easy? Because it was clear to them that they came up front with nothing—they were not the owner. After that, I thank them and let them sit back down with the hundred dollars. They are often shocked that I would really give them the hundred dollars. But then I remind them that it's not mine anyway—that I am only the manager. Now they, rather than I, have become the manager of it.

Interestingly, one time when I did that illustration, I had a person who felt irritated that I was so glib with "the church's money." I reassured them that the money used was from my own wallet, not from the offerings of the church. I also tried to help them see that my entrusting a hundred dollars to someone to manage was just a drop in the bucket compared to what God gives to each of us throughout our lives. Yes, the volunteer can walk away and blow the money on any number of worthless things. Or they can be a perceptive manager handling it now in view of the coming future. The point is that the same is true with us.

HOW SHREWD ARE WE, REALLY?

Collectively, Christians are much more generous in charitable giving than those who profess no faith. However, on average we give only 2.5 percent of our income as charitable giving (including all giving to the local church).[3] Before we slip into thinking that it is because we do not have enough money, let's remember that this generation of Americans is wealthier than any other previous generation, yet during the Great Depression, Christians gave 3.3 percent of their income to charity.[4]

What could happen if every American Christian decided to take decisive action now in view of the coming future much like the shrewd manager did? Just for the sake of discussion, let's say we moved from giving 2.5 percent to a full 10 percent for Kingdom purposes. That additional 7.5 percent would mean an additional $165 billion per year would be available to use.

That $165 billion per year has the potential to radically change the world as we know it. We could relieve global hunger, starvation, and deaths from preventable diseases in five years. That would cost $25 billion. Another $12 billion would eliminate illiteracy in five years, and $15 billion would solve the world's water and sanitation issues, specifically at the places in the world where one billion people live on less than a dollar per day. Some researchers estimate that another $1 billion would fully fund the great commission. All that good could happen and still leave another $110 billion for additional ministry expansion and further care for the national and global poor.[5] If more American Christians accepted Jesus' call for us to be shrewd managers, decisively acting now based on our coming future, this present world would be drastically different.

Apparently, so would our future one. Jesus makes this intriguing statement: "I tell you, use worldly wealth to gain friends for yourselves, so that when it is gone, you will be welcomed into eternal dwellings" (Luke 16:9). Scholars and theologians have debated exactly what Jesus meant by that. Whatever our speculations on how it integrates within Jesus' other teachings, it is clear that what we do now with the wealth we are assigned to manage matters in eternity.

In commenting on this parable, Jesus did not warn us not to *have* resources; he warned us not to *serve* wealth (see Luke 16:13). One of the joys of life is having resources that we have been given to manage for God's glory, our good, and the benefit of others. The idea is not that we go hungry while others are full. This is what God's Word tells us in another place:

> Command those who are rich in this present world not
> to be arrogant nor to put their hope in wealth, which
> is so uncertain, but to put their hope in God, who
> richly provides us with everything for our enjoyment.
> Command them to do good, to be rich in good deeds,
> and to be generous and willing to share. In this way they
> will lay up treasure for themselves as a firm foundation
> for the coming age, so that they may take hold of the
> life that is truly life.
>
> I TIMOTHY 6:17-19

THE JOY OF GIVING YOUR SHOES AWAY

A number of years ago, I was having a cup of coffee with a young adult at a local coffee shop. We were on a covered outdoor patio adjacent to the sidewalk. It was cold and raining, a rare occurrence in Los Angeles. As I was seated on the patio, I could see a guy stumbling down the sidewalk. It was clear that he was homeless. Los Angeles has a lot of people who are homeless. Ashamedly, my self-talk that day was that I hoped he was not going to come onto the patio asking for money. When you live in an area with a lot of panhandling, it can become wearisome to constantly be asked for money. Or at least that's what I am tempted to tell myself.

The man did come onto the coffee shop patio. He asked several other people for money, and they all ignored him. He came to our table and asked us for money. My friend did not have his wallet. I had treated him to the coffee. I did not have any cash either, just my credit card.

Then my friend asked the man what he needed the money for. The man—who I'll call David—said he needed it for shoes. It was only then that we looked down and saw his dirty, misshapen feet with bruises and cuts all over them. He said that walking on the streets of Los Angeles with no shoes is very hard on his feet. We could now see that.

My friend invited David to sit down for a moment. He asked him what size his feet were. Size eleven. My friend then said, "Well, David, you are in luck. I do not have any money on me, but I do have size-eleven shoes. It sure looks like you need them more than I do. Plus, I have another pair back at home." My friend then unlaced his tennis shoes and got down on his knees to put his shoes on David's grimy feet as the man sat in the chair next to me. As this was happening, the hubbub of a coffee shop patio filled with coffee drinkers died down as jaws began to drop. Some people elbowed other people to turn around and see what was happening.

What they saw was my friend giving his shoes away. Joyfully. It might seem like a small thing, but not all acts of obedience have to be big. Plus, before we brush my friend's act off as no big deal, the reality is that David probably had asked many other people for money and was still left without shoes until he met my friend. Shoes on his feet were a very big deal to David.

David thanked my friend with a big smile. My friend told him that the shoes were just a small reminder to David that God loved him. David then moved on with his new-to-him shoes. My friend finished the rest of the coffee conversation barefoot. I still vividly remember walking out to the car, in the rain, with my friend in his bare feet.

I felt a mixture of regret for my own internal dialogue when I first saw David coming down the sidewalk, and inspiration by my friend's everyday act of simple generosity and love.

I also recall feeling as though I wanted to keep growing so I would not miss out on such simple yet holy moments like this for all the future Davids that God might bring across my path. My self-talk that day had been about growing weary of being asked for things. As a result of that, I was not prepared to take any real action. Thankfully for David, my friend was a wise, generous, and faithful manager that day.

The choice to be such a manager is a daily choice. None of us will live forever. Being shrewd, generous, and faithful starts now, with whatever amount God has currently commended to you. Whatever wealth we have now will one day be gone. So may we take a lesson from the shrewd manager and the words of Jesus, who said, "I tell you, use worldly wealth to gain friends for yourselves, so that when it is gone, you will be welcomed into eternal dwellings" (Luke 16:9).

If we do, this story has the power to change our everyday lives.

CHAPTER 9

WHY EVIL EXISTS NOW BUT WON'T FOREVER

The Story of the Wheat and Weeds

Poor God, how often He is blamed for all the suffering in the world.
It is like praising Satan for allowing all the good that happens.

E. A. BUCCHIANERI

I believe that unarmed truth and unconditional love will have
the final word in reality. This is why right temporarily defeated
is stronger than evil triumphant.

MARTIN LUTHER KING JR.

AS A PASTOR, I have heard people give two main reasons for not
being active in the local church: (1) people in the church seem just
as lousy as everybody else, and (2) with so much evil and suffering in
the world, belief in a good and loving God is a tough pill to swallow.
For the first charge, they usually cite some sin they assume they are
innocent of and assume people in the church are guilty of, whether
it be racism or greed or hypocrisy. For the second charge, they usually cite some evil that they ascribe to God's ineptitude.

The implication of these charges is that if God and Christians
could each clean up their acts, just think of all the people we could
get into the church. The only problem with this is that the news
headlines tell us every day that the world is even more of a mess
than the church may be, even with all the church's imperfections.

This desire to get things sorted out and cleaned up is a near universal human desire not just limited to conversations about the church. Case in point, the United Kingdom held its local elections not long ago. A brand-new political party won its first seat. The name of this newly founded party?

The Rubbish Party.

Rubbish is the United Kingdom word for garbage, waste, and litter. The goal of the party is to get rid of the rubbish they see all around them.

From time to time, the church has certainly tried to clean up both its act and God's act, though this has never quite been pulled off: "Let's get rid of the deadwood and cut this thing down to the really committed, really good people." It has been said that such attempts often end up creating a church full of people who look more like those who crucified Jesus than those who followed him. It is like the old saw about two Puritans talking to each other and one of them says to the other, "There is none so righteous as me and thee, and sometimes I worry about thee."

You do not have to live very long to ask a cluster of questions regarding the problem of evil. Why are there evil and dangerous people in the world? Why doesn't God just get rid of them? And how are we supposed to handle them while we are waiting? One day Jesus addressed that exact set of questions.

THE GOODNESS OF GOD AND THE EXISTENCE OF EVIL

Here is another story Jesus told: "The Kingdom of Heaven is like a farmer who planted good seed in his field. But that night as the workers slept, his enemy came and planted weeds among the wheat, then slipped away. When the crop began to grow and produce grain, the weeds also grew.

"The farmer's workers went to him and said, 'Sir, the field where you planted that good seed is full of weeds! Where did they come from?'

"'An enemy has done this!' the farmer exclaimed.

"'Should we pull out the weeds?' they asked.

"'No,' he replied, 'you'll uproot the wheat if you do. Let both grow together until the harvest. Then I will tell the harvesters to sort out the weeds, tie them into bundles, and burn them, and to put the wheat in the barn.'"

MATTHEW 13:24-30 (NLT)

Do you understand Jesus' story? If not, don't feel bad, because neither did his closest followers. They walked by fields of wheat every day, and they still had to ask him what the story meant. Here is Jesus' explanation:

Leaving the crowds outside, Jesus went into the house. His disciples said, "Please explain to us the story of the weeds in the field."

Jesus replied, "The Son of Man is the farmer who plants the good seed. The field is the world, and the good seed represents the people of the Kingdom. The weeds are the people who belong to the evil one. The enemy who planted the weeds among the wheat is the devil. The harvest is the end of the world, and the harvesters are the angels.

"Just as the weeds are sorted out and burned in the fire, so it will be at the end of the world. The Son of Man will send his angels, and they will remove from his Kingdom everything that causes sin and all who do evil. And the angels will throw them into the fiery furnace, where there will be weeping and gnashing of teeth. Then the righteous will shine like the sun in their Father's Kingdom. Anyone with ears to hear should listen and understand!"

MATTHEW 13:36-43 (NLT)

HOW DID WE GET HERE?

This story helps make some sense of the problem of evil and its existence in a world created by an all-powerful, good God. The farmer's plan was good seed in his good field. It alludes back to Genesis, where God saw all that he originally created and that it was very good. It was an enemy who distorted the farmer's good plan.

Jesus' words here of "everything that causes sin" and "all who do evil" do not refer to people who drive fifty-eight in a fifty-five-miles-per-hour zone. In the story, it is clear that there is an enemy of God. Some people choose to live lives of such consistent evil that they are known as "children of the devil" (1 John 3:10).

These are literally Satan's seeds.

These people not only sin but also cause others to sin. It's the person who turned your now addicted son on to drugs. It's the person at work spreading lies about you because he or she doesn't like you and wants your job. It is the person who has been hitting on your spouse. It is the guy who buys a trafficked girl for a night of his pleasure at her pain. We are talking about the people whose lives are all about doing whatever they want and not caring if it hurts other people.

Why will Jesus remove them? Because Jesus hates the suffering they create in others. God is going to put an end to it. They will either change or be removed. The world is a mess now, but it won't be forever. Jesus wants justice to be done and people to be protected and live in joy. In the story, he says, "The righteous will shine like the sun in their Father's Kingdom" (Matthew 13:43, NLT).

God's plan for an all-good world has been temporarily delayed but not ultimately defeated. But let's not sugarcoat this. Not everyone will be included. There will be a fiery furnace and the gnashing of teeth.

JUSTICE REQUIRES JUDGMENT

Many people are not conscious of the fact that Jesus' teachings included such confrontational ideas. For those aware of it and raised in a Western culture, we have been schooled to be troubled by this point of Jesus' words. My nonbelieving friends say to me, "I like this Jesus guy, but can't I have all the 'love one another' stuff without these words about fiery furnaces and gnashing teeth?" In a word, no. If God is loving, then he must desire justice, which requires judgment. As author and preacher Max Lucado observes, in our culture, "we disdain judgment but we value justice, yet the second is impossible without the first. One can't have justice without judgment."[1]

Still others familiar with the violent images of this parable may wonder, *Isn't asking people to believe in teachings like this just going to cause them to be more violent?* You'd think so, but it's just the opposite in real life.

Miroslav Volf is a Yale professor who is from Croatia. Life in the early 1990s in Croatia was unthinkable. People would come and literally kill your children and burn down your house. Volf argues that if you do not believe in a God who punishes evildoers, then when someone comes into your home, kills your children, and burns down your house, what are you going to do? You would do that and more to those who did that to you.

But let's say you do believe there is a God who will punish and remove the evil. Then you don't have to take matters into your own hands. The need for such a belief to restrain revenge sounds severe if you've never lived in a place of extreme violence against you. Volf writes,

> The only means of prohibiting all recourse to violence by ourselves is to insist that violence is legitimate only when it comes from God. . . . It takes the quiet of a suburban home for the birth of the thesis that human nonviolence corresponds to God's refusal to judge. In a scorched land, soaked in the blood of the innocent, it will invariably die. And as one watches it die, one will do well to reflect about many other pleasant captivities of the liberal mind. . . . If God were *not angry* at injustice and deception and *did not* make the final end to violence God would not be worthy of our worship.[2]

Divine retribution is not just practical doctrine that restrains revenge in our down-to-earth world; it's also what this parable of Jesus teaches.

WHICH ONE DO YOU PULL UP?

We want to get rid of dangerous and evil people now. The sooner, the better.

Our natural instinct is to think, *God, why don't you just get rid of them now? Or if not, let us.* Here's why God doesn't want that: "If you try to tear out the weeds, you'll tear out the wheat" (see Matthew 13:29). What does Jesus mean by this?

When we think of a weed, we might think of a dandelion or

other common weed. The word Jesus uses, often translated "weed," is a specific type of rye grass called darnel, which has poisonous seeds. At the harvest, if you processed it with the good wheat, the resulting flour would be ruined. If you fed it to your family, they would get sick. So the poisonous weeds must be removed.

Here's the problem: Until they are full grown, darnel and wheat are virtually impossible to distinguish from each other. You might think you are removing a weed, when you are really uprooting wheat. The reason Jesus does not ask us to get rid of evil people is that we would not do a very good job of it. We keep thinking someone is a weed. We write the person off. We look down on the individual and wish he or she were simply gone. God is saying, "Be patient. Give that person some time and you might be surprised. That person might turn around." It was the same with the parable of the two sons: One looked obedient in the morning but proved disobedient, and vice versa for the other.

Let's pretend you had the job of uprooting some people and leaving others. The first case goes like this: In his teens, he began living with someone. He got her pregnant. After living with her fifteen years, he dumped her and got engaged to someone else. He got engaged to the second woman only because doing so would advance his career. During his two-year engagement, he began living with a third woman, who was not his fiancée. Meanwhile, he joined a cult. He eventually became bored with that and became a skeptic.

Leave him rooted or pull him up? Looks like a weed, but if you tear him out, you tear out the future Saint Augustine, one of the most influential and important Christians in history.

We are not the judge, as we do not have all the information to make a just judgment. Thankfully, we can trust that God's judgments *are* just.

GOD'S RESTRAINING WORK WHILE WE WAIT

Now, you might be thinking, *So how are we to handle evil? Are we supposed to just let it run rampant?* No. God is at work restraining evil even while the ultimate solution for getting rid of it lies in the future. God has given us his Word as a moral standard (see Psalm 119). He has created the family to bring up children in the instruction of the Lord (see Ephesians 6:1-4). He has founded the church to be the light in the midst of darkness and the pillar and foundation of the truth (see Matthew 5:14-15; 1 Timothy 3:15). God's Holy Spirit is now present to restrain the growth of evil through convicting the world of sin and of the coming judgment (see John 16:8).

Limiting evil now is one of the reasons God has instituted human government (see Romans 13:1-7). Part of the role of a police officer, a CEO, a governor, an army officer, a principal in a school, or a senior pastor in a church is to enforce law and order within an assigned domain. Yet because there are such things as unjust laws, we are not absolved from actively calling for our laws and leaders to be as just as possible within this world.

God has given us authorities to punish evil people and restrain them from doing more. Authorities should discipline, arrest, expel, or confine evil people to jail if necessary. Jesus' parable is not denying that; it is simply observing that no matter how much we do that here and now, there are still going to be evil people. The farmer will sooner or later separate the wheat from the weeds, but not fully in this moment while the harvest is still growing.

TRUSTING WHILE WE WAIT

How then should we respond to the suffering we experience from the evil that is present with us?

First, don't be surprised when you suffer (see 1 Peter 4:12-19). Just because you suffer does not mean that God has abandoned you. Sometimes suffering comes because wheat is surrounded by weeds. It is comforting to know that God will bring full justice later, but suffering is part of this world until then. This is not to claim that our present world is the best of all possible worlds. The parable makes it clear that the best of all possible worlds lies ahead, not now. Yet, our present world is the best way to the best possible world, even with our suffering now. In their book *When Skeptics Ask*, Norman Geisler and Ronald Brooks write,

> If God is to both preserve freedom and defeat evil, then this is the best way to do it. Freedom is preserved in that each of us makes our own free choice to determine our destiny. Evil is overcome in that, once those who reject God are separated from the others, the decisions of all are made permanent. Those who choose God will be confirmed in it, and sin will cease. Those who reject God are in eternal quarantine and cannot upset the perfect world that has come about. The ultimate goal of a perfect world with free creatures will have been achieved, but the way to get there requires that those who abuse their freedom be cast out.[3]

Second, we should expect to receive a reward when we suffer for God. One of the disciples who heard this parable of Jesus later wrote, "Even if you suffer for doing what is right, God will reward you for it. So don't worry or be afraid of their threats" (1 Peter 3:14, NLT). As Jesus says in the explanation of the story, the day of reward is coming when "the righteous will shine like the sun in their Father's Kingdom" (Matthew 13:43, NLT).

Third, pray to be protected and delivered from evil. Jesus prayed for the protection of his followers: "My prayer is not that you take them out of the world but that you protect them from the evil one" (John 17:15). And he taught his followers to pray for deliverance: "Our Father . . . lead us not into temptation, but deliver us from the evil one" (Matthew 6:9, 13).

Last, decide not to take revenge. Do you dare trust that God will settle the score for those huge, specific wrongs that were done to you? If you do, then you can be freed from the poisonous need to get revenge. You can move on with God's help and trust him to take care of it.

The teaching of this parable is captured in another part of the Bible, when we are told, "Dear friends, never take revenge. Leave that to the righteous anger of God. For the Scriptures say, 'I will take revenge; I will pay them back,' says the LORD" (Romans 12:19, NLT). Or as Volf argues, "The practice of nonviolence requires a belief in divine vengeance."[4]

Just because we cannot always understand God's plan does not mean he does not have one. Author Ravi Zacharias once was in India visiting the place known for making the best wedding saris in the world. A sari is a garment worn by Indian women and usually requires a length of cloth six yards long. Wedding saris are works of art; they are rich in gold and silver threads, resplendent with an array of colors.

During the visit, each sari was being made by a father-and-son team. The father sat on a platform two to three feet higher than the son, surrounded by several spools of thread—some dark, some shining. The son did just one thing. At a nod from his father, he would move the shuttle from one side to the other and back again.

The father would gather some threads in his fingers and nod once more, and the son would move the shuttle again.

This would be repeated for hundreds of hours until a magnificent pattern emerged. All along, the father had the design in mind and brought the threads together. God our Father has a fascinating design for each of our lives, but it requires that we trust him enough to keep our focus on him and respond to him at every nod.[5] Like the son in the making of the sari, we may not fully understand or know the exact details of the plan that is unfolding. God never promises us full comprehension of everything. He does, however, call for us to trust him in the things we cannot completely understand (see Philippians 4:7).

Jesus explains that the harvest in this story is at the end of the world. We can wonder what is taking so long, but we know that Christ is not really being slow about his promise to return: "No, he is being patient for your sake. He does not want anyone to be destroyed, but wants everyone to repent" (2 Peter 3:9, NLT). We can think of wheat and weeds as fixed categories, but when we let the camera pan back to take in the whole of Jesus' teachings, it is clear that there is a way for weeds to become wheat.

And that is not just good news for other people; it is good news for us, too.

NOT JUST "THOSE PEOPLE OUT THERE"

Let's not kid ourselves. Even we "good" people have quite a bit of evil running through us. As Aleksandr Solzhenitsyn observes, "The line dividing good and evil cuts through the heart of every human being."[6] Given how clear Jesus is here that sin and evil will eventually be permanently removed, we do well now to be ruthlessly urgent in our own dealing with the evil we see within our own hearts. If God let us do what we wanted and we could immediately get rid of all evil people, it would rid the world of not only the people who are 80 percent evil but also the people who are 8 percent evil. Are we so good that we are ready for that? If we have any self-awareness at all, we get quiet in a hurry.

But here's the best part: God created a way for our "weedy" souls to be changed into wheat. In his creative genius, Jesus paved the way so that when God destroys evil, he does not have to destroy us. It is called grace. It's the grace of salvation and the grace of sanctification, as we are created anew in Jesus for good works he's created in advance for us to do (see Ephesians 2:8-10).

This grace comes to us when we place our faith in Jesus Christ—when we know that our only real hope for true inner goodness comes from him. It is not just the offer of a second chance; it is the offer of a second birth (see John 3:1-21; 2 Corinthians 5:17). Because of this, we can become new versions of ourselves who no longer desire to do evil or cause others to sin, characterizations of our previous "weedy" ways. But now by God's work in us, we gain "the desire and the power to do what pleases him" (Philippians 2:13, NLT). As we live out the new "wheat-y" nature given to us by faith in Christ, when the harvesttime comes to remove forever from this world all that causes sin and all who do evil, God does not have to remove us.

Though temporarily delayed, God's great plan for a world without pain, sin, or evil will not ultimately be defeated. It's coming. We just have to wait. Why? Because God wants as many people as possible to be gathered into the new heavens and new earth, including people from every tribe, tongue, and nation.

Including me. Including you, too.

CHAPTER 10

RISING HOPE IN TROUBLED TIMES

The Stories of the Mustard Seed and the Yeast

> Faith is confidence in what we hope for and
> assurance about what we do not see.
>
> **HEBREWS 11:1**

> One person can change the world.
>
> **ROSA PARKS**

I AM NOT A GREAT RUNNER.

I learned this a number of years ago at the Rose Bowl. The Rose Bowl is the iconic football stadium in Pasadena, California. Surrounding the stadium is a three-mile loop where people walk and run seemingly all hours of the day and night. On this particular day, as I arrive at the loop, I tell myself, *I am not going to walk it today; I am going to run the whole three miles.*

You know how some people really love to run? They talk about the "runner's high." They will say that running is a great stress reliever for them. These are the people who can run and talk to their running partner at the same time. Do you know these people? I know these people too. Let's just say that I do not like those people. They make me mad. I am married to one of those people.

As I step out of my car, I have my running gear on. I'm all psyched up: I can do this! I have not run three miles in a while, but today is the day to do it again. About one mile in and all my psyched-up adrenaline is gone, and the willpower that was enough to *get* me going is not enough to *keep* me going. At this point, my commitment to try to run the Rose Bowl loop becomes all pain, challenge, and disappointment.

My side hurts and I start rationalizing quitting: If God wanted me to run, he would have built me like a gazelle instead of a fire hydrant. At that moment, there is this Rose Bowl–loop regular who jogs with a long bar of weight across his shoulders. That guy goes running by me—with about fifty pounds of weight on his shoulders!

Just then a new mom passes me. I can tell she is a new mom because she is pushing what seems to be a two-hundred-pound jogging stroller with triplets in it. The triplets look as if they were born two days ago. She goes breezing by me. But my humiliation is not done.

Then another person goes running by. What catches my eye about this man is that he is wearing construction boots, jeans, and a flannel shirt. I could handle being passed up by Hercules and Supermom. At least they both had on athletic gear. But being outpaced by a guy in boots, jeans, and a long-sleeved shirt is pretty disappointing.

So I quit running. I give up.

I walk about ten steps, and then another guy, a total stranger, goes running by me. He must have seen me quit. As he runs by, he turns his head toward me and says, "C'mon. C'mon." That's all he says. He doesn't slow down or stop running. He just keeps jogging.

For some reason, his simple encouragement on top of the fact that I am now running with a companion rather than alone makes me start running again. Life is a race. You don't get extra points for speed, but you do for endurance. And endurance requires hope.

Jesus told us two short down-to-earth stories to give us the courage we need to overcome disappointments in life with the power of hope. Here are the stories:

> He said therefore, "What is the kingdom of God like? And to what shall I compare it? It is like a grain of mustard seed that a man took and sowed in his garden, and it grew and became a tree, and the birds of the air made nests in its branches."
>
> And again he said, "To what shall I compare the kingdom of God? It is like leaven that a woman took and hid in three measures of flour, until it was all leavened."
>
> LUKE 13:18-21

Mark's version adds this:

> With many similar parables Jesus spoke the word to them, as much as they could understand. He did not say anything to them without using a parable. But when he was alone with his own disciples, he explained everything.
>
> MARK 4:33-34

THE HOPEFUL KINGDOM

The whole concept of a kingdom was very well known in Jesus' day. There were kings and kingdoms throughout history. The people had a certain set of expectations about how kings and kingdoms worked, usually that they centered on big displays of splashy power. Of course, Jesus displayed some of that in the forms of various miracles and other such high-wattage events, yet the Kingdom of God does not function on only such things.

God is at work. His Kingdom has come and is coming. It starts out extremely small and from an unlikely source. It is often hidden and unseen, but the Kingdom is spreading. One day all evil will be totally overcome and creation will be redeemed. People can endure the loss of many things—finances, careers, relationships, self-esteem, and even loved ones—and still continue onward. Nevertheless, there is one thing human beings cannot survive without: hope.

Hope is how we live. It is the air we breathe to lead spiritual lives. It gets us from one day to the next and sustains us in the dark times. You go to school in the hope that you will one day graduate and enter into a career. If you are single and want to be married, you go on dates with the hope that the process will lead you to finding the right person to share your life with. Often the hope of having kids sets in. When you have a child, the only thing that sustains you through the dark days of diaper changing is the hope that a day will come when things will be better. We volunteer time and give money to worthy causes because we hope it will make a difference.

When hope is gone, endurance, joy, energy, and courage all evaporate. Case in point, in 1952, Florence Chadwick attempted to swim the chilly ocean waters between Catalina Island and the California shore.[1] It is a distance of approximately twenty-six miles. She swam through foggy weather and choppy seas for fifteen hours. Her muscles began to cramp, and her resolve weakened. She begged to be taken out of the water, so aides lifted her into a boat.

They paddled a few more minutes, the mist broke, and Florence discovered that the shore was less than eight hundred yards away. "All I could see was the fog," she later said. "I think if I could have seen the shore, I would have made it."[2]

In fact, two months later, she tried again, hoping for better weather with no fog. However, once again the fog set in, only this time she kept a mental picture of the shoreline in her mind as she swam. With the picture in her mind of what she knew to be true, this time she made it all the way to shore!

Hope gives us the power to press forward.

The issue for life is this: *Are you putting your hope in the right thing?*

Biblical hope is not based on how things will specifically work out in your life on earth; it is based specifically on the hope of the one who promises to work in all things for the good of those who are called according to his purpose (see Romans 8:28). Jesus says to put your hope in the Kingdom of God because one day his plan for the universe will prevail, and this hope will never disappoint. Be careful not to place your hope in your assumption that you know what form the Kingdom of God will take. Otherwise, you may stand before a king crucified as a criminal on a cross and say, "Certainly, this has nothing to do with the coming of the Kingdom of God."

Prejudices about how the Kingdom *should* work will make God's greatest triumph look like his greatest failure to you.

BIG ENDINGS START WITH SMALL BEGINNINGS

The first of these two parables is an agricultural metaphor. A mustard seed was famous in Jesus' day for being incredibly small. Only one millimeter across, it is barely visible. However, when it is planted, it can create a plant that grows to twelve feet high in one season. Under ideal conditions, exceptional plants can reach thirty feet tall with a twenty-foot spread among its branches.[3] From this tiny, unlikely source comes this flourishing tree that can provide food and housing to many birds. Irresistible growth trumps small beginnings. Once the seed gets into the right kind of soil, it's only a matter of time.

The second story is an analogy of a woman baking bread. Unleavened bread is hard, dry, and unappetizing. She puts in only a little bit of leaven. A chemical process then occurs and the dough fills with thousands of little pockets of carbon dioxide. As the bread heats, each pocket expands. Soon the whole loaf grows and the entire house is filled with the aroma of fresh bread.

What is striking to Jesus' listeners is the amount of bread he's talking about. She's not making a single loaf or even two loaves; she's using sixty pounds of flour. Add some water, and you get enough dough to feed a lot of people—by today's standards, she's making roughly twelve hundred slices of bread! Jesus' original listeners were thinking what you are thinking: *You mean to tell me that all that dough can be changed by such a little bit of yeast?* Jesus says that a little bit of yeast in a great amount of dough, and it is only a matter of time.

Jesus uses a surprising action word to describe the baking process. He does not say the woman placed, sprinkled, or even mixed the yeast in the dough; he says that she *hides* it in the dough. You cannot even see it. That is the way the Kingdom works. It is not always readily recognizable to everyone. There is something hidden about it. The Kingdom starts with small beginnings in hidden ways but has unstoppable growth in time. The yeast has the power to change the dough; the dough does not have the power to change the yeast. The dough relies on the yeast. Thank God for the yeast!

A HOPE STRONGER THAN OUR DISAPPOINTMENTS

Jesus is telling these stories to people who suffer from disappointment. People had been hoping for centuries that God would act. The whole story of the Old Testament is the story of hope. People knew that this world was not the way it was designed to be. The same is true today. Maybe the only thing you can get people to agree upon is that things should be different.

After God's good creation, the Bible opens in the early stages with people choosing against God. They are banished from the garden, but before they leave they are given hope. A bit of hidden yeast, a millimeter-wide seed. God prophesies that the woman will have offspring and that the evil one will strike at his heel but that the offspring will crush the head of the evil one (see Genesis 3:15). This reference is to a future Messiah, sent by God to destroy the evil one and remove the curse. From the first chapters of the Bible, there is the seed of hope.

Then the Flood came, but God said, "Every time I see a rainbow, I will remember forever the covenant between God and every living creature. Never again will the waters become a flood to destroy all life" (see Genesis 9:12-16). Every time you see a rainbow, you will have hope. Hope was the manna that kept Israel going in the desert. Hope was the small voice whispering to Elijah that he was not alone even though he was convinced that he was. Hope was the message of future plans given through a discouraged preacher named Jeremiah who no one would listen to.

People waited and hoped, assuming that when the Messiah came, he would be a big, all-powerful king arriving with mighty armies to destroy all their enemies. The biggest enemy in Jesus' day was the Roman Empire. The people were waiting for a king to come and do something about the enemies. Jesus arrives and says the words they are waiting to hear: "The Kingdom of God is near!" (Mark 1:15, NLT).

This is it, they think. *The one who will crush the evil one is here. Let's crush their heads and start with ransacking Rome!* Some leave everything and follow Jesus. Many more watch closely to see what will happen. What they see is a traveling rabbi with a not-very-impressive band of followers. There's periodic teaching, a few healings, and that's about it. The rabbi doesn't build an army. He doesn't march on Rome.

Jesus knows that everyone will be tempted to think, *Is that all? This is the Kingdom?* Even John the Baptist is looking for more pizzazz. He basically asks Jesus, "Is this it, or should we expect someone else to come?" (see Matthew 11:3). Jesus responds by essentially saying, "Don't be confused, misled, or discouraged. The Kingdom of God has invaded this earth. It might look like the size of a mustard seed; it might look crude and utterly insignificant in the helpless manger, located in a backwater town called Bethlehem, but once it gets off the ground, it's only a matter of time."

But how much time? We do not know, and that's the challenge.

Once the yeast is in the dough, you cannot stop its force, so don't get discouraged now. Don't quit now. Evil will be overcome. The curse will be overthrown. Sin, guilt, and death will be destroyed. God's community will be redeemed and flourish. All creation will be renewed to what its status was before the curse. It might be foggy now, but keep a picture of the shoreline in your mind and take one more stroke.

WHAT DOWN-TO-EARTH HOPE DOES

We can mistakenly think that future hope is so heavenly minded that it does no earthly good. Nothing could be further from the truth. Assured future hope gives us down-to-earth power for today. Hoping while living in this world is not easy. The dough is not bread yet, and that's the hard part. So what does hope do now in this world?

First, hope waits patiently. Imagine for a moment how astonished the original disciples would be if they were brought back to earth today. We have the advantage of being able to see more than the original listeners. We can see that much has happened since Jesus originally told his parables. Continents they never knew existed are now filled with people who follow Jesus. There are hospitals and schools, inspiring art and music, reformed prisons, and more ethical businesses all because of God at work through Christians spreading the good works of God's Kingdom. The yeast is at work. The seed is growing.

We live between hope and fear. Sometimes it seems we can switch camps in the blink of an eye. It is easy to be tempted to give up and give in. Consider the case of my friend Herb Rodgers. He went to Bible college. He received a call to occupational ministry. However, his first wife left him. Ripped his heart out. He eventually went to seminary and married a woman named Jill. Jill then got sick with Parkinson's disease. Herb's days consisted of working at his job and then going home and working there for Jill. They would never have kids.

If you asked Herb, "What sustains you?" he would not talk about optimism in medical progress, as great as that is. He would not talk about his courage or his will. He would talk to you about Christ-centered hope. What is that? Christ-centered hope says that flaws in DNA will not get the last word.

Jill has since passed away. But Christ-centered hope says that one day Herb and Jill will walk and run. Christ-centered hope says the day will come when damaged bodies will be without pain or flaws and will know a glory for the ages that we cannot now even imagine. As Scripture declares, "If our hope in Christ is only for this life, we are more to be pitied than anyone in the world" (1 Corinthians 15:19, NLT).

Second, hope says it's just a matter of time. My wife and I have followed the time-honored tradition of those who grew up in Pittsburgh by brainwashing our children to love the Pittsburgh Steelers. Many years ago, when our oldest son, Caleb, was just four years old, he declared in the middle of a close Monday-night game that he was going to root for the other team to win. With a little parental coaching, he changed his mind back to rooting for the Steelers. And then whenever we would watch a game together, he would ask me, "Daddy, does our team win?" Usually, I had to say something like, "I don't know, buddy. We will just have to watch and see."

However, one day things were a bit different. I was sitting in the living room watching a recording of the previous season when the Pittsburgh Steelers won the Super Bowl. As I was watching the game, Caleb came into the room and sat down to watch some of the game. As usual, he asked me, "Daddy, does our team win?"

For once in my life, I could see the beginning from the end. And I have discerned that knowing that my team ultimately wins it all makes the whole season a lot more enjoyable to watch. So when Caleb asks, "Daddy, does our team win?" I can confidently answer, "Yes, Caleb. No matter how bad it might look right now, I know that in the end, our team wins."

Jesus' down-to-earth stories of the yeast and the mustard seed are his answer to our soul question "Does the Kingdom of God win?" Does evil have the last word, or does God hold the final say? Jesus answers, "The seed is in the ground. The yeast is in the dough. It's only a matter of time."

HOPERS WHO PASS ON OUR HOPE

Hearing these parables provides us with hope. But that is not the end. Bound up within the stories is the dynamic that when we hear them, they can become part of us. Like the yeast in the dough, the parables can be hidden in our hearts (see Psalm 119:11) and remind us of the unstoppable hope we have even in troubled times.

We need not hoard the hope we have received from Jesus' parables. Peter, one of the disciples who heard this parable, said, "Do not be frightened. But in your hearts revere Christ as Lord. Always be prepared to give an answer to everyone who asks you to give the reason for the hope that you have" (1 Peter 3:14-15). In fact, each time we share about the hope we have in Christ, we do our part to help the seed flourish and the yeast to create another pocket of air in the dough. We don't just consume hope and encouragement in Christ; we pass it on. That's what Jesus' disciples did by recording these parables for us. It is what Jesus expected when he told them to go into all the world and make disciples of all nations. If these parables offer us a hope that is worth having, it is then a hope that is worth sharing.

Remember the opening story, in which I started to run but then quit, only to have a stranger jog by telling me to "C'mon. C'mon"? I still had a long way to go to complete the Rose Bowl loop, and the cramp in my side was still present, but for some reason, his simple encouragement and the fact that I was now not running by myself made me start running again.

The jogger at some time turned off to go to his car, so I was again running alone in the spread-out crowd. Ahead of me was a guy who was all by himself and struggling to keep running. I watched him slowly give up and quit. I jogged up from behind and passed him on the right-hand side. As I did, I looked at him and just said, "C'mon. C'mon." And I kept jogging. After about ten more steps, he had caught up to me, and we finished the rest of the loop together.

Jesus originally told this chapter's two parables to help people who were suffering from disappointments in life. Disappointments are still part of life. That's why these stories are so relevant for us, too. Our disappointments with life are real. They are hard. They are scary. And they are also temporary.

These short stories give us the hope we need to run our races. They give us the reason to pass that hope on to the others God brings across our path. When we share that hope with others, we not only tell of these stories but also become part of them. We take up our part in spreading the Good News of the hopeful Kingdom of God to those around us as we wait patiently and hopefully for the final fulfillment of the Kingdom, when the tree is fully grown and the bread fully baked.

Be encouraged.

It will happen.

The seed is in the good soil. The yeast is in the dough.

It is only a matter of time.

CHAPTER 11

HOW TO BE A HERO

The Story of the Good Samaritan

God has chosen us to help one another.

SMITH WIGGLESWORTH

If you can't feed a hundred people, then feed just one.

MOTHER TERESA

IT WAS JUST ANOTHER DAY for Cameron Hollopeter.

The twenty-year-old film student was waiting on a platform in the New York City subway station. Out of the blue, he began to suffer a seizure and fell to the ground. He then struggled to get back up again, staggering uncontrollably along the platform edge. People could hear the train rumbling through the subway tube toward the station. And then the unthinkable happened: Just as the train was about to arrive, Cameron fell from the edge of the platform onto the tracks.

People stood helpless, frozen with fear and shock. Others cringed and turned their heads. In mere moments, a young man would meet an unthinkably violent end because he had a seizure at the wrong time in the wrong place and no one could stop it.

Except the one man who did: Wesley Autrey.

Wesley, a fifty-year-old construction worker, was on the platform that day with his two daughters, ages four and six. He was on his way to drop them off with their mother before heading to work. Wesley said, "I had a split-second decision to make. Do I let the train run him over? . . . Or do I jump in?"[1]

He jumped in.

The headlights of the train were bearing down on them. Unable to hoist Cameron back up to the platform, Wesley threw him into a twelve-inch drainage trough between the rails and dived on top of him to pin him down. Disoriented and confused, Cameron continued to struggle with his hero. The train driver saw the men and slammed on the brakes. But it was moving too fast, so it ran right over the top of the two men, with less than two inches to spare between them and the bottom of the train.

The men were eventually both freed unharmed from their space underneath the train. Wesley Autrey was hailed a hero. But he would have none of it: "I don't feel like I did something spectacular. I just saw someone who needed help."[2]

Yes, but others can see there is something heroic when we do so.

AN UNEXPECTED HERO

Jesus once told a parable about coming to someone's rescue:

On one occasion an expert in the law stood up to test Jesus. "Teacher," he asked, "what must I do to inherit eternal life?"

"What is written in the Law?" he replied. "How do you read it?"

He answered, "'Love the Lord your God with all your heart and with all your soul and with all your strength and with all your mind'; and, 'Love your neighbor as yourself.'"

"You have answered correctly," Jesus replied. "Do this and you will live."

But he wanted to justify himself, so he asked Jesus, "And who is my neighbor?"

In reply Jesus said: "A man was going down from Jerusalem to Jericho, when he was attacked by robbers. They stripped him of his clothes, beat him and went away, leaving him half dead. A priest happened to be going down the same road, and when he saw the man, he passed by on the other side. So too, a Levite, when he came to the place and saw him, passed by on the other side. But a Samaritan, as he traveled, came where the man was; and when he saw him, he took pity on him. He went to him and bandaged his wounds, pouring on oil and wine. Then he put the man on his own donkey, brought him to an inn and took care of him. The next day he took out two denarii and gave them to the innkeeper. 'Look after him,' he said, 'and when I return, I will reimburse you for any extra expense you may have.'

"Which of these three do you think was a neighbor to the man who fell into the hands of robbers?"

The expert in the law replied, "The one who had mercy on him."

Jesus told him, "Go and do likewise."

LUKE 10:25-37

The people listening to Jesus knew this road well. Roughly eighteen miles long, it connected Jerusalem to Jericho. The road was notorious for being narrow and full of twists and turns. Even today, the road is known as the "Red and Bloody Way" because so much violence has occurred there.[3] It was easy for thieves to slip in from the surrounding desert wilderness, assault and rob someone, and then disappear back to the desert.

In the story, the man was left there, beaten and half-dead. Thankfully for him, a few others were traveling the road that day. The first was a priest. He would have been at the top of the religious leadership of his day, presiding over worship of the nation of Israel, keeping the traditions alive. We are not told why, but the priest passed by. Next came a Levite. He would have been similar to an associate pastor. He also did not take the time to stop.

The original listeners would have surely expected each of these two men to stop and render aid. Why didn't they? Jesus does not tell us, and maybe that alone makes the point. Whatever justifications they might offer do not matter. They probably had their reasons for not stopping. We know this because we often face the same temptation and challenges in our own lives.

OVERCOMING FEAR TO LOVE OUR NEIGHBORS

The first obstacle we face when it comes to loving our neighbors is fear. We often teach our children at a young age about "stranger danger." What is beneficial thinking for a child is not always a helpful way to think as an adult, yet we often carry that childhood warning with us throughout our adult lives. Perhaps the priest and Levite thought the situation was a ruse. What if they stopped to help and it was just a scam, with robbers waiting to attack each of them? Our fear about what will happen to us if we get involved is one of the biggest inhibitors to loving our neighbors. It is cleaner, easier, and safer to stay disengaged—to be indifferent.

But indifferent people never make a difference.

SLOWING DOWN TO LOVE OUR NEIGHBORS

If not fear, then we are confronted with the tyranny of the urgency of our schedules. Time pressure can become a moral category for us. Perhaps the priest and Levite felt pressed to make it to an important meeting they were expected to be at. I know this can be true from my own life.

A few years ago, I was headed to a young-adult retreat that I was scheduled to lead. Retreats are always an amazing time with God, but they are often pressure packed for the leaders. There are countless logistics that need to be managed. Plus, there is the added weight of the sincere desire to see a breakthrough in the lives of people who have made the decision to come to the retreat.

That day, I was headed from Los Angeles to our local mountains with a lot to do as I prepared to welcome hundreds of young adults to the retreat starting later that evening. Suddenly, the freeway traffic slowed from a horrific accident that had just occurred. Like the priest and Levite, I did not see the event, but I did see the aftermath. There were no ambulances or sirens.

There was a man staggering in a confused and agitated state near a vehicle that was upside down in the far-right lane. He must have been ejected from the car. This is a bit graphic, but much of the skin on the left side of his face had been destroyed from sliding across the pavement. Next to him was an elderly woman who had pulled over to try to help him. She was having a hard time because he was a big guy. My first thought was *I need to stop and help her with him. She can't handle him alone.*

True-confession time. This was my second thought: *I really don't have time for this right now. Depending on how long I am delayed, I might not get to the retreat in time to lead it. I have literally hundreds of people counting on me.* For whatever reason, my better impulses prevailed. It's not lost on me that they prevailed partly because I knew the story of the Good Samaritan. It was in me. The only question was whether it would be lived out by me. I stopped and helped calm the man and kept him safe until an ambulance arrived.

Rushing to leave, the elderly woman stopped me and said, "You know, hundreds of cars drove by without stopping to help. Maybe they all thought I had it handled. What made you stop?"

I told her, "I know you might think this is weird, but I stopped because I know that Jesus loves that man and he needed help."

She said, "When I saw him, he was stumbling around on the road. I knew he needed help. But I was afraid because I know I am quite frail in my old age. I thought he might unintentionally hurt me in his confused state."

Now she had me interested in how she overcame her fear and decided to help, so I asked her. With a delightful twinkle in her eye, she responded, "You might think this is weird, but I stopped because I know that Jesus loves that guy and he needed help."

It's not just priests or Levites of old who can be tempted to pass by and hurry along with internal justifications in mind. That can happen to me and you, too. Pressure can do that to us.

Years ago, researchers at Princeton University did a fascinating experiment based on this parable. They told seminary students that they needed to go across campus to another building. One group was told they were to prepare a talk about the parable of the Good Samaritan. To vary the felt urgency in the schedule, the researchers told one group that they were running late in making it across campus and told the other group they had a few minutes but should get moving anyway.

Along the way, the students passed a man sitting slumped in a doorway who moaned and coughed twice as they walked by. Unknown to the students, the moaning man was simply an actor playing the part. What the researchers discovered was that a person in a hurry is less likely to help people. This was true even of the students who were going to the other building to speak on the parable of the Good Samaritan! Some literally stepped over the victim on their way to the next building. People in a hurry, hurry by people. Their results seemed to show that simply thinking about helping does not mean we will actually do it. We can be educated beyond our obedience. It also demonstrated that as the speed and pressure in our lives increase, our ethics suffer.[4] As author Dallas Willard once said, to be a better follower of Jesus, we "must ruthlessly eliminate hurry" from our lives.[5]

OVERCOMING SKEPTICISM TO LOVE OUR NEIGHBORS

Even when fear for our safety and lack of time do not keep us from loving those in need, our skepticism can. Our thoughts can quickly jump to how they might misuse what we offer rather than to what we might offer that they could use. Skepticism can keep our guard up, which keeps our compassion down.

The needs of our neighbors can be much more than only economic, but imagine you pass a person with a sign asking for money. Living in an urban area, I am not oblivious to the fact that some people prey upon the generosity of others. That is a tragedy because it hardens our hearts to those genuinely in need. However, the greater tragedy is to help no one to avoid being taken advantage of by someone.

Instead of allowing our skepticism to determine *if* we help, we can use it to helpfully shape *how* we help. For example, instead of giving money, we can walk with the people to a store to purchase the food they need. Sometimes slowing down can humanize our neighbors as we get to know their names as we walk together to meet their need. However, this may not always be possible. Keeping gift certificates with you for a nearby restaurant chain can be a wise way to meet the need without allowing skepticism to justify doing nothing.

Our built-in suspicion can impede our willingness to love our neighbors on a larger level. But maybe we could love our neighbors not only through individual acts of love but also through more systematic ways. So now in addition to loving one specific homeless neighbor, we decide to give our time, money, or resources to a homeless shelter. Yet that same skepticism can seek to thwart our moving forward with this plan. *What if the organization does not steward my donation well? What if my time is wasted?* Of course, there are ways around this, too, because we can often learn about the organization's track record of stewarding past resources given in advance of giving them ours.

Skepticism can even begin to shape our perceptions of the person in need, with little evidence to support it. Perhaps the priest and Levite saw the man bloodied on the side of the road and concluded, "He probably deserved it." They could have presumed foolishness on the part of the man in need: "Well, he probably was carrying a large sum of money, and everyone knows you cannot do that on this road." There is nothing in Jesus' parable that communicates that someone's past foolishness, even if actual, alleviates us from the responsibility to act lovingly.

Countless times I have heard people tell me that homeless people in Los Angeles "just need to get a job." The rationalization goes something like this: "They are homeless because they are lazy, so why should I help them?" Yes, able-bodied and able-minded people in need should do what they can to improve their situations (see 2 Thessalonians 3:6-12). However, a high percentage of people experiencing homelessness suffer from mental illnesses of one form or another. Telling a person with debilitating paranoid schizophrenia to simply get a job is not always realistic. To the point, John Claypool observes, "Once a person is robbed and beaten and lying by the side of the road, elaborate speculation on how he got there is secondary to doing something about his wounds."[6]

HOW TO BE A HERO

With the priest and Levite now having passed by, Jesus continues the parable. Most of his listeners certainly thought the third character would be just a regular, non-clerical Jew. Had he done that, Jesus would have made the listeners into the heroes of the story.

In a radical twist, the third person is a Samaritan. First-century Jews regarded Samaritans as loathsome and evil people. The Samaritans practiced a heretical version of Judaism and were ethnically distinct from the Jews. People of that day would not have expected any humane, heroic, or compassionate response from a Samaritan.

The Samaritan, presumably riding his donkey on the road, discovers the beaten man. He stops, gets off his donkey, and does what he can to help him. Apparently, sometimes we have to get off our donkeys to make a difference. He takes him to the nearest inn, where the wounded man would have long-term care. The Samaritan pays for all this out of his own pocket and promises to pay for any extra expenses.

This is a parable about loving our neighbors as we love ourselves, yet Jesus never tells us much about the Samaritan's feelings. In our world, we use the word *love* to mean many things. In the same breath, we can say that we "love" tacos and then turn around and say that we "love" our family members.

When Jesus talks about loving our neighbor, he is not mainly talking about feelings; he is talking about action. Theologian N. T. Wright captures this well:

> As often in Jewish and Christian thought, "love" is first and foremost something you do, not something you feel; the feelings often follow the actions, not (as in some modern thinking) the other way round. . . . What "love" means, first and foremost, is taking thought for someone, taking care of them, looking ahead in advance for their needs, in the way that you would take careful thought about, and plan wisely for, your own life.[7]

In other words, love does.[8]

Jesus' teachings show that many times action leads the heart. Authentic love does not come from only our feelings. Our feelings are not the only part of us. We also have our wills. Speaking about money (which the Samaritan had to have as well as use, as part of his love for his neighbor), Jesus says, "Where your treasure is, there your heart will be also" (Matthew 6:21). Sometimes feelings follow the determination to do an act of love. Authentic feelings of indifference can be transformed by a genuine will to make a difference.

The Samaritan's guarantee of paying any extra expenses incurred in the care of the hurting man is an important detail. In Jesus' day, there were no credit cards. The man clearly had just been robbed, so he would not have had any cash. If the amount to nurse him back to health was more than what the Samaritan had paid, the owner of the inn would have been legally obligated to sell the man into slavery as a debtor, as the man would not have had the money to cover the debt. It was the law of the day. The Samaritan is guaranteeing that the man will be not only healthy but also free. Loving our neighbors can often require some thoughtful consideration about all their needs, not just the immediate ones.

All this talk of loving our neighbors can sometimes sound like we are talking about a legalistic, works-based salvation. The best succinct summary found in the Bible on how grace, faith, and good works are designed by God to all come together in our lives is found in Ephesians 2:8-10:

> It is by grace you have been saved, through faith—and
> this is not from yourselves, it is the gift of God—not
> by works, so that no one can boast. For we are God's
> handiwork, created in Christ Jesus to do good works,
> which God prepared in advance for us to do.

Martin Luther put it this way: "Salvation is by faith alone, but true faith never remains alone."[9] Grace does not free us from loving our neighbors. Grace is when God saves us so we now desire to love our neighbors well.

Thankfully, many Christians have taken this call to love our neighbors seriously. In fact, this is the mission of the number one nonprofit hospital network by size in the US, Ascension: "Rooted in the loving ministry of Jesus as healer, we commit ourselves to serving all persons with special attention to those who are poor and vulnerable."[10] It started with just a few of Jesus' followers trying love their neighbors well. It's nonprofit, but last year its revenues were higher than that of Facebook, Starbucks, or Southwest Airlines. Additionally, four of the five largest nonprofit hospital networks in the US are run by Christians trying to live out Jesus' concern for the poor and vulnerable.

It's not just hospitals. Sociologists have shown that local churches create what is called a halo effect, with both social and economic uplift to the area, including to many people who are not part of the congregation.[11] It's amazing what can happen when each follower of Jesus takes seriously his commands. Of course, not every act of loving our neighbors will be noteworthy. As Fred Craddock once pointed out,

> Most of us will not this week christen a ship, write a
> book, end a war, appoint a cabinet, dine with the queen,
> convert a nation, or be burned at the stake. More likely
> the week will present no more than a chance to give a
> cup of water, write a note, visit a nursing home, vote for
> a county commissioner, teach a Sunday school class, share
> a meal, tell a child a story, go to choir practice, and feed
> the neighbor's cat.[12]

Love does not have to be sensational to be love. Sometimes it is simply about being available and faithful.

WHAT KIND OF NEIGHBOR WILL I BE?

Availability and faithfulness are not necessarily dramatic, but they are inherently costly. This parable makes it clear that if we love our neighbors only when it requires no time, energy, money, or risk, we will never love our neighbors as ourselves. All love is costly. That is what Jesus showed us not just in this parable but in his own life when his love for the world led him to a Red and Bloody Way known as the Cross. He saw we were in need, and it was within his power to help us. Thanks be to God that he did not pass by.

Jesus finishes the story with a simple question: "Which of these three do you think was a neighbor to the man who was in need?" (see Luke 10:36). The answer is obvious, right? The one who showed mercy. Jesus says, "Go and do likewise" (verse 37).

Did you catch the significant twist Jesus makes? The lawyer starts with the question "Who is my neighbor?" In the beginning, it is asked from the perspective of who we are obligated to help. By the end, Jesus asks the question from the perspective of the man who was in need of the help.

"Who is my neighbor?" now has become "What kind of neighbor will I be?" What started as a discussion about the nature of other people has now become an unanswered question of our own nature. That's the power of these stories: They are complete in their telling yet incomplete in their effect until we decide how we will respond to them. Jesus doesn't make his original listeners (or us) the heroes of this story. Instead, he invites us to *become* heroes, only this time it's in the stories of our own neighbors who are in need.

Love your neighbor as yourself. And who is your neighbor? Your neighbor is anyone who is in need that you are in the position to help. It is as straightforward and as challenging as that. So now, in line with the point of the parable, what kind of neighbor will you be?

CHAPTER 12

WELCOME HOME!

The Story of the Prodigal Son

Nothing but God's Grace! We walk upon it; we breathe it; we live and
die by it; it makes the nails and axles of the universe.

ROBERT LOUIS STEVENSON

A simple word of greeting, an offer of a cup of coffee on me, a smile and
a hug will all go a long way toward reconciliation. A listening ear can
open a wandering heart to the thought that God still loves them, and
there just might be a place still set for them at their Father's table.

KATHERINE J. WALDEN

LEGEND TELLS OF A MAN who had a wild and reckless son. The
young man became friends with the hooligans of the town and was
eventually persuaded to join them in robbing his very own father's
house. After the burglary was over, his friends made a fast getaway
with the loot, leaving him to be caught by the authorities. He was
left to face the guilt of the crime alone.

The young man was distraught. He not only betrayed the trust
and love of his father but had also brought public dishonor to
the family name. In a culture in which family honor is the highest good, this was the worst wrong of all. Desperate and deeply
repentant, he went to his father, begging forgiveness. Graciously,
it was granted.

The father called on all the extended family members to

celebrate the return of his son. Everyone enjoyed a grand banquet. Near the end of the celebration, the father stood and lifted his cup of rice wine for a toast. The son drank deeply of his cup but then suddenly grabbed his throat and fell dead across the table. The son had been poisoned.

The father, with ceremonial dignity, nodded to the guests. Each returned the gesture by politely bowing to the father as they silently left the dinner hall. All was now put right. The son had paid the price of his pardon with poison. His honor had been restored. The family integrity and public name were returned. The whole unfortunate incident was now closed.[1]

THE POWER OF THE RIGHT
KIND OF FATHER

That is certainly one way that a father could respond. Jesus gives us a completely different picture of how God the Father relates to his children. It is one of his most famous stories. It also featured a wild and reckless son, but that's where the two stories part ways.

There was a man who had two sons. The younger one said to his father, "Father, give me my share of the estate." So he divided his property between them.

Not long after that, the younger son got together all he had, set off for a distant country and there squandered his wealth in wild living. After he had spent everything, there was a severe famine in that whole country, and he began to be in need. So he went and hired himself out to a citizen of that country, who sent him to his fields to feed pigs. He longed to fill his stomach with the pods that the pigs were eating, but no one gave him anything.

When he came to his senses, he said, "How many of my father's hired servants have food to spare, and here I am starving to death! I will set out and go back to my father and say to him: Father, I have sinned against heaven and against you. I am no longer worthy to be called your son; make me like one of your hired servants." So he got up and went to his father.

But while he was still a long way off, his father saw him and was filled with compassion for him; he ran to his son, threw his arms around him and kissed him.

The son said to him, "Father, I have sinned against heaven and against you. I am no longer worthy to be called your son."

But the father said to his servants, "Quick! Bring the best robe and put it on him. Put a ring on his finger and sandals on his feet. Bring the fattened calf and kill it. Let's have a feast and celebrate. For this son of mine was dead and is alive again; he was lost and is found." So they began to celebrate.

LUKE 15:11-24

THE FATHER WHO IS PRESENT AND ACTIVE

Jesus presents the Kingdom of God with the image of God as a Father who is present, active, and involved, not absent, passive, and removed. If we don't make that observation, we will not understand the full chain-breaking power of this story. When Jesus came, the most common image he used to refer to God was that of Father. He could have used the imagery of a therapist, life coach, general, caesar, or CEO. But he chose the word *Father*. That tells us something.

The Bible tells us that "no one has ever seen God, but the one and only Son, who is himself God and is in closest relationship with the Father, has made him known" (John 1:18). So Jesus came with the specific purpose to make God the Father known. He came to make known not just that God exists but also what he is like.

The impact of our fathers is staggering, including how it affects our faith formation. Almost every famous atheist had a father who abandoned, abused, or disappointed him or her deeply. It was true of Adolf Hitler, Mao Zedong, Friedrich Nietzsche, David Hume, Madalyn Murray O'Hair, Bertrand Russell, Sigmund Freud, Jean-Paul Sartre, Albert Camus, H. G. Wells, and Ludwig Feuerbach, just to name a few.

Psychology professor Paul Vitz shows how these and other famous atheists all had fathers who were absent or unloving.[2] Our fathers have the power to influence us profoundly for good or evil (sometimes without our even knowing it), not just in our physical DNA but also in our starting point for our understanding of faith.

It's important to note that just because a person starts out with the obstacle of an unhelpful father does not mean he or she will not come to know God in a real and personal way. Case in point, apologist and evangelist Josh McDowell, whose father was a violent alcoholic, once said it this way: "I grew up believing fathers hurt because my dad hurt me."[3] It was not until years later that he was able to separate the disappointment and pain he felt regarding his biological father to see a clear picture of God as our heavenly

Father. It was then that he moved from being an "ornery agnostic" to a follower of Christ.[4]

I have many memories of my dad being present, active, and involved in my life while I was growing up, including at family dinners, on vacations, around the house, and at my various sports games. I still remember the time the umpire didn't show up for our Little League baseball game and my dad ended up filling in. On one of my at bats, he called me out on a called third strike. Clearly, his eyes must have been going bad at that point in his life. He was a good dad, but not perfect! My dad always told me how much he loved me and how proud he was of me, and he never let me become too cool to hug him. Maybe your experience with your dad was like mine.

Or maybe your experience was different. My wife's dad walked out the door when she was only one year old. I recall the lunch where she met him for the first time after more than thirty-three years of absence. Suffice it to say that Jesus knows that not all dads give us clear pictures of what he means when he calls God *Father*. The prodigal-son parable helps clarify that.

When I spend time with my three children, I do not ask them if they believe in God. I know that they already do. I ask them where they have seen him active and present in their lives. I am trying to help them develop the eyes to see that just like the father is present and active in this story, God is also present and active in their stories. He's like that in my story, and yours, too.

It may be fair to ask if that's a realistic jump. Just because Jesus had a father so present and active, can we automatically conclude that he meant for us to make that connection to our own lives? Absolutely. Remember, that's the whole point of the parables. They are told by Jesus to be "thrown alongside" our own stories.

The parables are not just curiosities; they are corrective lenses for our hearts' visions of God the Father and life within his Kingdom. Jesus came to make God the Father known. Using parables is one of the ways he does that.

THE FATHER'S SCANDALOUS GENEROSITY

With the father present in the story, the question becomes "What is he like?"

Jesus answers this initially by the father's response to the younger son. The son's asking for his inheritance prematurely is essentially telling his father that he cannot wait for him to die. He wants the money now. This is an unheard-of level of entitlement.

Astonishingly, the father divides the property between his two sons. In Jesus' day, the firstborn son was due a double portion of the inheritance. So the younger son presumably jets off with a third of the estate. Jesus' listeners would not have known which was more scandalous: the son's request or the father's response. Under no obligation to honor this hurtful request, the father still chooses to do as requested. The word *prodigal* means lavish.[5] As many others have observed, maybe we should call this parable the prodigal father instead of the prodigal son.

Every day we choose between two alternatives: living with the father or using our free will to depart for a distant land. The first option is to do life with God. We stay present to God, who chooses to be present and active with us. We bring every low to him and celebrate every high with him. His deepest desire is for us to live at home with him, trusting that the best is with him, not away from him.

LIFE IN A DISTANT COUNTRY

There is another way to do life: far from the Father. We choose this when we find sin more attractive, often because our perception of the Father is so skewed. We can doubt that his restrictions and guidelines exist because he has our best in mind. We are confronted with this choice not once but regularly. We can choose what the younger son chooses, as the band Imagine Dragons concludes in the hit song "Whatever It Takes": "I'm the prodigal son. I was born to run."[6]

Of course, life in the distant country is fun at first. Otherwise, it would not be a temptation. However, eventually the fun departs but the pain, guilt, and shame remain. We lose an inner sense of freedom. We also lose our outer freedom as our unrestrained life choices lead to the carnage of failed friendships, broken finances, and even emotional or physical health problems, depending on the choices made. We can feel anxious, threatened, and paralyzed by fear. Instead of seeking sustained joy, we search for momentary bursts of pleasure.

The younger son loses all of his share of the estate through his wild living. God will honor our free will, even when we go against his will. We are free to choose, but we are not free to select the consequences of our choices. Sometimes that truth is learned only the hard way.

Paralleling our own tendencies with those of the younger son, author and theologian Henri Nouwen says,

> Our addictions make us cling to what the world proclaims
> as the keys to self-fulfillment: accumulation of wealth
> and power; attainment of status and admiration; lavish

consumption of food and drink, and sexual gratification without distinguishing between lust and love. . . . The addicted life can aptly be designated a life lived in "a distant country." . . . Beneath it all is the great rebellion, . . . the unspoken curse: "I wish you were dead."[7]

Now sitting with the pigs, things have hit rock bottom. The Jews considered pigs to be an unclean animal. The pods that the pigs were eating even began to look appealing to the prodigal son. Jesus is teaching us that when we spend enough time away from the Father's house, our appetites adjust. We start to call good what we once thought of as gross.

Part of the brilliance of Jesus' stories as a way to teach is that they have the power to touch on so many areas of our lives at once. His listeners both then and now are forced to confront where their appetites have adjusted. Spending enough time away from the Father, we too can start to call good what once was believed gross. Life in the distant country is always marked by the moral relativism that pig food is just fine for us these days.

Then notice what Jesus says: "But no one gave him anything" (Luke 15:16).

Jesus is giving us a picture of direct contrast to the father's generosity.

GOD'S ABILITY TO USE OUR PAIN FOR OUR PROGRESS

The pain of his hunger coupled with his remembering his father's generosity makes the younger son come to his senses. Sometimes we need pain to make a spiritual breakthrough. As C. S. Lewis astutely noted, "Pain insists upon being attended to. God whispers to us in our pleasures, speaks in our conscience, but shouts in our pain: it is His megaphone to rouse a deaf world."[8]

Deep souls rarely grow without seasons of pain.

All of us have seasons of pain in our lives. If you have not had one of those, just keep living and you will! Maybe you are in one of those right now. It very well could be an area of pain through which God wants to work in you. His Word promises that he will work in all things—not just the good things—for those who love him and are called according to his purposes for them (see Romans 8:28). Your painful season in a relationship with a friend might be how God teaches you to rely on his presence in greater ways. Or maybe he will teach you how to be a better friend to others. Maybe you have the pain of feeling unfulfilled inside or a financial debt that is depressing you. It could be pain over sin in your life.

What will you do when you reach the pain? Will you allow it to become the catalyst for renewed thinking, or will you try to numb it and let it drive you further into the distant country? The hunger pains led the son to renewed thinking, which led to the trek back to the father's house. He's going back hoping for the "hired-servant plan," sure the "son plan" has been forfeited by his foolishness.

THE GOD WHO RUNS

Jesus reveals a father who does not give up on his rebellious son. He sees his son a long way off, presumably because he has daily scanned the horizon in the hope his son would come to his senses and return. Seeing him, the father runs to his returning son. This is a culturally humiliating act. In that day, it was believed that important people do not run to others; others run to them.

In the first century, if a Jewish son lost his inheritance among the Gentiles and then returned home, the Jewish community would perform a specific ceremony. It was called the *kezazah* and was designed to humiliate the returning son. Members of the community would break a large pot in front of him and yell, "You are now cut off from your people!" and he would be totally rejected forever.[9] The father is running to protect the son from the village. In other words, the father is humiliated so that the son is not.

Is that the picture you have of God the Father? Because that is the very picture Jesus wants to inject into your life. He is not like the father in the opening story, who was more concerned about the family reputation than the well-being of his son. This father couldn't care less what anyone in the village thinks. In Jesus' parable, all that matters to the father is his starving, aching, exhausted son who wished him dead. His undeserved humiliation takes the place of our deserved humiliation.

The son did not even have the chance to finish his prepared speech before he was given the good gifts of a robe, a ring, sandals, and a celebration. There was no poison at this banquet. The ring was the symbol of his authority; the shoes were the mark of being a free man, not a slave. This son had returned from the land where no one would give him anything and come back to the father who was prepared to welcome him home with everything (see Luke 15:22-24).

That's God's heart toward you. Whoever you are, wherever you have been, whatever you have done, God is waiting for you to come home. And when you do, he will sprint to you, embrace you, kiss you, and welcome you. That is the heart of the Father whom Jesus came to make known.

We might be tempted to wonder why the father did not just go to the distant land and find the son. At the very least, he could have sent some of his servants to force the younger son to return. But this misses the point that Jesus is giving us. It also shows that the father will not force the son to be in relationship with him; it must be chosen freely. And so it is with God and us, too.

The best storytellers know that the art of storytelling means saying no to some possibilities in order to say yes to others. The story takes shape not just by what is included but by what is intentionally excluded. Yet the absence of some detail in a parable is not necessarily a theological assertion by Jesus. The parables are prophetic and pastoral: prophetic because they are designed to get past our defenses to help us see our lives as they are; pastoral because they call us to make any needed changes to live in light of the story told. We wrestle with seeing what is there and not getting sidetracked by what is not there.

A DISTANT HEART CLOSE AT HOME

Jesus continues the parable, now bringing the older son into the story:

> Meanwhile, the older son was in the field. When he came near the house, he heard music and dancing. So he called one of the servants and asked him what was going on. "Your brother has come," he replied, "and your father has killed the fattened calf because he has him back safe and sound."

The older brother became angry and refused to go in. So his father went out and pleaded with him. But he answered his father, "Look! All these years I've been slaving for you and never disobeyed your orders. Yet you never gave me even a young goat so I could celebrate with my friends. But when this son of yours who has squandered your property with prostitutes comes home, you kill the fattened calf for him!"

"My son," the father said, "you are always with me, and everything I have is yours. But we had to celebrate and be glad, because this brother of yours was dead and is alive again; he was lost and is found."

LUKE 15:25-32

The context for this story gives us a notable insight. When interpreting parables, it is essential to know not only the story but also the context. Though many lessons are learned through the front part of the parable with the younger son, Jesus actually is focused on the father and the older brother. We know this because what prompts Jesus to tell this parable is that "the tax collectors and sinners were all gathering around to hear Jesus. But the Pharisees and the teachers of the law muttered, 'This man welcomes sinners and eats with them'" (verses 1-2).

The younger brother forces us to consider whether we will live close to the father or in a distant land. The older brother forces us to reflect on whether we've chosen to live close to the father, but our hearts have become hardened toward the mercy of God shown toward others. If we are not careful, we can end up wanting mercy for ourselves and punishment for others. We may not want *kezazah* for ourselves, but that does not always mean we don't want that to happen to another.

We can be lost in a distant land, but we can also be lost right at home. The older brother's heart is a million miles away from the father's heart of mercy. The older son refuses to go in, so the father goes out seeking him. That is the heart of the father, always looking for his children. Jesus is showing us that whether we have lived wildly or coldly, the father's desire is for us to be reunited with him.

FINDING YOURSELF IN THE PARABLE

To find your way forward in your own story, you have to locate yourself within *this* story. This is how God uses these parables to do his work in our lives. This parable is so multifaceted that we may find ourselves identifying with different people within the story, depending on what part of our stories we reflect upon.

Maybe God is using this parable to help you see that your earthly father was not the best picture of your heavenly one. If absence, pain, or disappointment were your experience, I am sorry for that. Genuinely.

Jesus tells this parable in part to make God the Father known. If you have children or hope to one day, you can break the cycle of pain and be part of God's outworking of redemption by being the kind of parent your parents may not have been to you. Be present, active, involved, generous, and merciful.

Maybe you are seeing yourself in the story as the younger son in a far-off country. You picked up this book because you were wondering if Jesus had a down-to-earth story to help spark hope in your life. If so, can you see that the Father is ready to run to welcome you home? How does that happen? Through Jesus. He didn't just come to tell us stories; he came to change ours. Do not wait another moment. The ring, sandals, the robe, and a celebration are waiting for you!

Maybe you are not the prodigal son but you know one. Perhaps you can't help but think of how your child, a friend, or other loved one is doing life far from God. You can be encouraged by knowing that their story is not over yet. God is still in the business of welcoming prodigals back home.

Of course, this parable may instead cause you to identify with the older brother. Maybe you have grown resentful toward those who have lived wildly, only to return to be fully welcomed back into the father's house. Do not live another moment outside of the party. Ask God to make your heart tender again toward him and his mercy. Ask him to help you remember all the times he has been merciful to you as well. What was lost is now found; what was once dead is now alive again. Such resurrective power has already launched the celebration. The fattened calf is going to be eaten whether we join the party or not. In the parable, the father tells the older son, "Everything I have is yours" (verse 31). That means the ring, sandals, the robe, and a celebration is waiting for you, too, if you are willing.

CHAPTER 13

THE CREATIVE POTENTIAL OF A SOFT, DEEP, UNCLUTTERED HEART

The Story of the Four Soils

Even more blessed are all who hear the word of God and put it into practice.

JESUS, LUKE 11:28, NLT

The Word of God is like a lion. You don't have to defend a lion.
All you have to do is let the lion loose, and the lion will defend itself.

CHARLES SPURGEON

THEY CALL IT THE MOSQUITO.

It is a cell-phone ring tone that high school students use to keep their teachers from discovering they are using their phones in class. The pitch of the ring tone is too high for many people over twenty-five years old to hear,[1] so students text each other during class without the teacher knowing.

It was first developed to keep students from loitering outside convenience stores, which was apparently scaring away older customers. The stores play this tone over an outdoor speaker. Set as a constant tone, it was annoying enough that students would no longer loiter in front of the stores. But now it's been turned into a ring tone that students are downloading in droves. More than a hundred thousand of them crashed the company's website trying to download the ring tone at once.

How does the mosquito tone go undetected by adults?

Inside our ears we have tiny microscopic hairs that are moved by incoming sound waves. Those hair movements send electrical signals to our brains. As we age, those hairs get worn down, so our hearing becomes less sensitive. We first lose the ability to detect sounds of high frequencies. To give you some scale, the highest note on a piano is four kilohertz.[2] Many people over age twenty-five can't hear sounds above sixteen kilohertz.[3] The mosquito tone is seventeen kilohertz.[4]

Jesus tells a story about four soils to the gathered crowd. Intriguingly, he starts the parable by telling us to listen. He then concludes it by saying that if we have ears, we should listen. It is like he is saying, "Despite having ears on the outside of your head, you might miss what I am saying to you if you don't grow some spiritual ear hair." If we cannot hear what he is saying, we will miss out on the good things God wants to grow in our hearts and lives.

> Jesus began to teach by the lake. The crowd that gathered around him was so large that he got into a boat and sat in it out on the lake, while all the people were along the shore at the water's edge. He taught them many things by parables, and in his teaching said: "Listen! A farmer went out to sow his seed. As he was scattering the seed, some fell along the path, and the birds came and ate it up. Some fell on rocky places, where it did not have much soil. It sprang up quickly, because the soil was shallow. But when the sun came up, the plants were scorched,

and they withered because they had no root. Other seed fell among thorns, which grew up and choked the plants, so that they did not bear grain. Still other seed fell on good soil. It came up, grew and produced a crop, some multiplying thirty, some sixty, some a hundred times."

Then Jesus said, "Whoever has ears to hear, let them hear."

MARK 4:1-9

HEALTHY THINGS GROW

This parable is about growth, which is a normal sign of health. I have three children, and I remember the nervous joy of bringing each of them home from the hospital. The joy was centered on the wondrous miracle of our newborn. The nerves were centered on paying attention to whether or not our baby was growing as he or she should.

Growth is a sign of health. Pediatricians actually use growth charts as a way to ensure that everything is functioning as intended on the inside of the child. In the initial stages, a crucial sign of health is that the baby begins to gain appropriate amounts of weight as the weeks pass. Outward growth is a sign of inward health.

However, pediatricians also have a term for a baby who is not growing: failure to thrive. Thriving is what is normal. It is what is expected if everything is working as designed and intended. It is what human beings were created to do: grow and thrive. When a baby does not grow, the doctors begin to search for the barriers that are keeping the baby from thriving.

Spiritually speaking, God wants us to grow and thrive. To love someone this week we could not love last week. To forgive someone this month we would not forgive last month. To share faith with someone today in a way that we would not yesterday. To be generous this week in ways that we were not last week. To pray more deeply, to trust more fully, to rejoice more fiercely, and to show compassion more freely.

When you see people who are growing like that, you sit up and take notice. They are not deaf to what God is saying to them. They listen, understand, and obey. They don't just hear the story; they hear what God is saying to them through the story. Their lives are marked by something deep, majestic, and beautiful. You and I are made for nothing less. When thriving happens, people around us take notice too.

This year the church I serve celebrated a decade of serving the at-risk kids in one of our local public elementary schools. The school identifies the kids who are struggling either educationally, behaviorally, or socially. We then match them with someone from our congregation who mentors the student one on one for one hour per week.

Over a recent cup of coffee, the principal of the school thanked me for all that the people of our congregation have done for the kids. She shared that she really does not understand what motivates our people, with all the demands of life, to show up in such large numbers every week. She may not understand it, but she can see it. She came to address our congregation at my invitation. She told us that in the school, our church is known as a "wave of love."[5] Jesus said that love would be the mark by which the world knows that we are following him (see John 13:35).

WE ALL HAVE A HEART CONDITION

Jesus constantly encountered people who were failing to thrive. They were choked by anger, paralyzed by fear, with hearts made small by sin and suffocated by hopelessness.

Scripture tells us that our hearts can deceive us and we need help to understand ourselves (see Jeremiah 17:9). Jesus comes to help us do just that. Because we can deceive ourselves so easily, he tells us this story as a tool to assess whether we are thriving and, if not, for us to ponder what might be the barrier stopping us from thriving as God desires for us. The purpose of this parable is not for me to judge others; it is for me to make a judgment on my own heart condition.

The story has three core elements to it: the sower, the seed, and the soil. When you listen to the parables of Jesus, always look for the element that changes to figure out what Jesus is driving at. For example, the seed does not change. It is not a story about good seed compared to bad seed. When later questioned on the parable, Jesus tells his disciples that the seed is the Word of God, which will always bear fruit if it is given half a chance in our hearts.

The sower also does not change in the story. It is not a story about a good sower or a bad sower. The sower is not stingy with the seed. He is generous with it to the point of extravagance. He gives all the different soils a chance; he's not careful or tight fisted in spreading the seed.

The variable, of course, is the soil. Whether or not the seed takes root and thrives depends on the soil's condition. You can count on the sower being good. You can count on the seed being good. It's the soil that changes the results.

I love corn on the cob. Fresh and sweet. It reminds me of

summer. This past year I decided to plant corn in my yard. I went to get some seed from the local nursery and asked the expert about how best to grow the corn. He said, "Well, you live in the right place. We get plenty of sun. But before you get started, you need to test your soil to make certain it's the kind that will let the seed do its thing."

With this parable, you can consider *soil* to mean your heart or life. Jesus is helping us test our soil. Is your heart in the condition that will "let the seed do its thing"? Although growth is normal, it is a mystery exactly how it happens. It is a gift from God. We cannot make growth happen, but we can prevent it.

HARD HEARTS: HOW IT HAPPENS
AND WHAT TO DO ABOUT IT

The first soil that the seed falls on is a path where the soil had become hard. Soil does not start out hard; something has to happen to it for it to get hard. In this case, either people or sheep walked on it and created a path. Jesus says for the seed to have a chance, the soil has to be soft, not hard. Open, not closed.

Jesus knows that it is easy to get hard hearts and deaf ears. Life has a way of hardening hearts. You get disappointed, stepped on, and hurt. We begin to form protective shells. We get defensive, cynical, and even bitter. So when the Word of God comes to us, it's not even given a fair hearing. It is not given a chance to enter in and do its thing. We do not want to hear it, sometimes because we know that it will mean that something has to change in our lives.

Someone who knew this well was a boy named Wolfhart Pannenberg, born in 1928 in Poland. During his years as a boy, Wolfhart had little interaction with the church or the Good News about Jesus. However, at the age of sixteen, he had an intense experience that he later called his "light experience."[6] Seeking to understand this experience, he began to search through the works of the great philosophers and thinkers.

A high school literature teacher who had been part of the portion of the church that stood against the Nazis in World War II encouraged Wolfhart to take a hard look at Christianity. He did just that, which resulted in his understanding that his "light experience" made sense only through the resurrection of Jesus Christ. Wolfhart went on to become one of the most prolific theologians of the twentieth century, once saying, "The evidence for Jesus' resurrection is so strong that nobody would question it except for two things: First, it is a very unusual event. And second, if you believe it happened, you have to change the way you live."[7]

For the first soil, we do not want to receive God's Word. It just lies there on the surface until the enemy comes to steal the seed. Is your heart soft, tender, and open to what God says to you? Or has it become closed and hardened toward him? Don't make the mistake of thinking that the soils are fixed in their current state. If that were the case, there would be no point in Jesus telling us this parable.

As mentioned in the introduction, the Hebrew word for "parable" means a riddle or puzzle. It means that you have a role to play. You have to think about the story. You have to wrestle with it. You have to have ears to hear and suddenly the lights can come on and you realize, *That is me. That is the condition of my heart.* That's when your spiritual ears wake up and start working again.

Imagine a theoretical conversation in which one person says to another, "You know, I have been thinking about you recently and have realized that you are hard hearted, defensive, and closed off." The other person says, "Wow. Thanks for pointing that out. What can I do to change?" How many times has that interaction happened in human history? Never!

That is why Jesus gives us a story. He is giving hard hearts a chance to realize, on our own, our condition. A person who comes to their own conclusion that their heart has become hardened is much more likely do something about it than a person who is just told by another that they are hard hearted. This story is a grace. It's a mercy designed to get past our own defenses—to honestly see if God's Word is really leading to good growth and good change in our lives.

You may discover that there is a hard spot in your heart. You have been hurt and now that pain has turned to bitterness and resentment. You may have had a dream that you worked hard to achieve and it crumbled, and the disappointment has built a shell around your heart. Hard hearts can happen when we put our very best into relationships that have fallen apart, so we tend to protect ourselves by believing the worst about people. If that is you, will you let God make you tender toward him again—open to him again?

Imagine if soil had feelings and it were given the option of being plowed. I think the soil would say, "I'll pass on that and stay hard. That way it will not hurt so much when I get stepped on again." Breaking up hard-packed soil is painful. It means having faith that the fruit that will come from a heart that returns to being tender to God's Word will be worth the pain. However, there is a pain greater than being plowed; it's the pain of missing out on what God's Word can do in our lives when we are tender soil open to it.

SHALLOW HEARTS: HOW IT HAPPENS
AND WHAT TO DO ABOUT IT

Jesus' parable has some of the seed fall on a second type of ground: shallow soil. Much of the land where Jesus told this story is a foundation of rock with only a couple of inches of topsoil. Roots that begin to grow immediately hit the rock and have no chance to flourish. Jesus says that growth requires soil that is not only soft but also deep.

A famous Los Angeles street artist once ironically said, in response to the assumption that people from LA are superficial, "It's not like they're wrong, but what they don't understand is, we're deeply superficial."[8] Shallowness is not just a condition of soils; it can also be the condition of our lives. As author Richard Foster once observed, "Superficiality is the curse of our age. The desperate need today is not for a greater number of intelligent people, or gifted people, but for deep people."[9]

We live in a shallow world. Our friendships are often built thumbs to thumbs rather than face to face. We like our food fast and our commitments short. But Jesus is saying, "Trouble will hit—a crisis, a loss, a pain. And when it does, if you've been running your life at warp speed, you will find that fast lives don't run very deep." The options are to lead either fast lives that are superficial or slow lives that are deep. But there is no fast-and-deep option available.

Constant busyness kills our spiritual ears. We live in a global culture that values constant change. We are told that the answer to pain is often more change. We feel pain, so we change jobs, marriages, life groups, churches, and friendships. We can keep changing in hopes that a change will bring the change we so want. However, once the adrenaline of the change is gone, we discover that nothing has really changed. If you visit a tree nursery, you'll find out that it is a precarious thing to take a thriving tree and try to transplant it. Roots require time and endurance to develop.

Through this story, Jesus asks us to reflect on how deep our lives are. Have we stayed somewhere long enough to develop deep community around us that we have stuck with through a painful experience or loss? Do we have people in our lives who we, without becoming automatically defensive, allow to speak to places where we need to change? Is there depth in your relationship with God? If you are a Christian, has your relationship with him gotten any deeper over the past year? He loves to answer this prayer: "God, I want to be deeply rooted. Help rid me of my shallowness."

CLUTTERED HEARTS: HOW IT HAPPENS
AND WHAT TO DO ABOUT IT

Some of the seed fell among a third kind of soil: areas with weeds and thorns. This soil is soft, deep, but cluttered. All the potential of the soil, all the nutrients, are being consumed by weeds, so the seed is choked out by the competition. This soil is not bad; it's unfocused. In trying to grow everything, it doesn't grow the one thing that will yield a harvest.

When it comes to Jesus' parables, it is important to not mix and match the interpretation of common images. These are not the same weeds from the earlier story of the wheat and weeds. Jesus tells us that those weeds in that parable represent everything that causes sin and all who do evil (see Matthew 13:41). He gives us the clue that the weeds in this story represent "the worries of this life and the deceitfulness of wealth" (verse 22), so they require a different approach.

The cluttered heart may be the most dangerous condition because it can be the subtlest. We can think, *My heart is not hard and I am not shallow, so I am fine.* A worried, cluttered heart can begin to think we can hoard our way to salvation. We must be careful that we do not end up with a houseful of stuff and a soul filled with emptiness.

About a year ago I was with a group of underground church leaders, most of whom live within a Muslim-majority country. The leaders were sharing about the explosive church growth despite the persecutions the people face from the government. One of the leaders had spent time in prison for his faith. He had actually been expelled from the country and now resided in the US.

I commented to the leaders that it must be hard to live as a Christian in their specific country. The leader who lived in both places responded, "Actually, Tom, after living in that country and now the United States, I think it may be harder to follow Jesus in the United States." I asked why he thought that might be the case.

He continued, "America enshrines the pursuit of happiness in its Declaration of Independence as the goal of life. But Jesus says you need to pick up your cross and follow him. If you have been taught that life is mainly about your own happiness, Jesus' command will either confuse you or offend you." God used this man's words to make me realize that I have some weeding to do in my life. Weeds do not just go away on their own. Even if you pull them out, unless you get the whole root, they will reemerge later.

It's subtle. You jump online for a moment and end up being there for an hour. Now the time you had planned to spend in God's Word is gone. Or maybe we need to do some financial weeding. We can become so concerned with keeping up with others that we are left with no financial margin. Then when Jesus calls us to be givers (see Luke 6:38; Acts 20:35), his word is suffocated.

As a father, I can see how the cares of this world can tempt us to lead such busy lives. We can become afraid that our kids will fall behind, so we enroll them in everything. Soon our lives are taken over by soccer, piano lessons, swimming, Little League, and clubs. These are not bad things; however, if they begin to block the chance for God's Word to be heard and responded to, then it's time to do some weeding. If the cares of this world lead you to try to be involved in everything, you end up deeply committed to nothing—not even the main thing.

Remember that corn I planted? Here's what happened to it: I put it in the ground and made certain it had good, deep soil. I set my automatic sprinkler to water it, and it started to sprout up. It grew quickly to about four feet in height, and I was delighted. It even started to grow some corncobs. I could not wait for the harvest to come.

But I got busy—too busy to pay attention to the corn.

Then my sprinkler tubes got clogged. Because I did not check on the corn due to my being busy, the sun scorched it and killed it. We never actually ate any corn from it. I missed the harvest because I was too busy, too distracted from what I was trying to grow. Missing the harvest of corn is one thing; missing the good harvest that God wants to grow in our lives is quite another.

THE CREATIVE POTENTIAL OF A SOFT, DEEP, AND UNCLUTTERED HEART

The final soil that Jesus tells about has incredible potential needing only God's Word to make it a reality. When his Word meets a soft, deep, uncluttered heart, we will thrive. The growth is unstoppable if the soil is right. God's increase will happen in us and through us when we let the seed "do its thing." And the increase will be beyond our wildest imagination: thirty-, sixty-, and a hundredfold.

Two years ago one of our church's international partners from Kenya walked into my office unfolding plans to expand the hospice center that she leads. This is an inspiring, remarkable, and trusted woman who had been sent out from our church years earlier. Her organization's track record with the first hospice center, which we had supported as a church, was strong. They do what they can to nurse people back to health. Those they are unable to nurse back to health are given dignity and hope in end-of-life care.

As she unfolded the drawings, she shared that the first phase of a second location, which would be used to care for those sick with HIV/AIDS and cancer, would cost about $1.2 million to build. The land was already purchased and the drawings already complete. She was just now beginning to try to raise the funds to expand their services done in Jesus' name to the least of these.

I asked her what amount she was asking for our church to give. She said she had no answer to that question. Her only answer was that she felt confident that God would provide for this work. I am pragmatic enough that I would tell almost anyone else that they needed to come up with a specific request for me to present to the elders of our church; however, my respect and admiration for this leader allowed me to accept her response.

As our elders were discerning how to respond to the plans, one of our elders came upon Proverbs 19:17 during his time of prayer and reading God's Word. It says, "If you help the poor, you are lending to the Lord—and he will repay you!" (NLT). The question was asked, "What would we give if we really believed this was true? What if we simply took God at his word?" The unanimous answer from the elders was that we would give the entire needed $1.2 million. We already had the money in a reserve account. We knew that our congregation would be excited by this decision, but it was also an act of trusting that God would take care of us, too, even with significantly less in our reserve account. We gave the $1.2 million so the work could begin immediately.

It has been about two years since that decision. In the coming months, I have the privilege of going to that country for the grand opening of the now completed hospice center that will care for all who need it for generations to come. Some who would have died without access to the care and medicine will now live. Others will still die, but they will not die alone or without dignity. All of this was possible because the leaders of the hospice organization kept their hearts soft, deep, and uncluttered, allowing them to hear God's leading for them to step out to develop a second location. Plus, our elder team kept our hearts open to simply take God at his word.

Yet even before that moment, there were many other moments when the thousands of people who call Christian Assembly Church their home kept their hearts soft, deep, and uncluttered to hear God's Word to be generous. Each person who gave back to God through our worship services made the decision possible. It was their generous giving that created the reserve fund in the first place. Without all their individual, smaller acts of obedience, the one larger group act of obedience never would have been possible.

It is astonishing what can happen when the soil of our hearts stays soft, deep, and uncluttered. And by the way, in the year that followed the night that decision was made, our giving increased by $1.7 million dollars above what it had been up to that point. In other words, God has more than repaid us for the gift to the poor, just as Proverbs 19:17 said. Even more, there is a harvest of good works and comfort for the sick that will be around for generations to come. That little piece of the world will genuinely be changed because some of Jesus' followers simply took God at his word and let the seed do its thing in the soil of their hearts.

SOILS THAT JOIN IN THE SOWING

Jesus told this parable to challenge as well as encourage his followers. If you are a follower of Jesus, you are both the soil and the sower. That's what happens with healthy things: They grow, they bear fruit, but they also spread more seed around them. At times, you will sow seed by sharing God's Word and people will be hard and nonresponsive. They may be shallow or cluttered. Jesus said that this will happen a lot and you'll be tempted to quit, but don't. A harvest will come.

Your job is to keep generously, lavishly spreading the seed of God's Word. You never know which heart the harvest will come from, so keep sowing. Your job is not to make the seed grow. It's not your responsibility to judge any soil other than that of your own heart. Farmers do not know how the seed grows; they just put it in the ground and it grows. Don't get discouraged. Look at Jesus and all the failures he experienced with people. He told his parable to a great crowd, but few stayed and followed him.

The religious leaders of Jesus' day, the people you would think should be most open, were often the most hard-hearted, bad soil. They plotted Jesus' death. His family questioned him. The Romans washed their hands of him. The crowds who once flocked to him would soon taunt him. His disciples deserted him. From the cross, Jesus had to think, *Did any of the seed take? Was it worth it, or was it all a waste?*

On the cross, one thief mocks him, exhibiting bad soil. But the other one asks Jesus to remember him, revealing that despite what his heart was like before that moment, it was now soft and open to Jesus. Even on the cross, the sower is still throwing seed. He just keeps sowing. He dies, but death cannot hold him down. He told his friends that unless a grain of wheat falls to the earth and dies, it remains a single grain of wheat. However, if it dies, it bears much fruit (see John 12:24). So do not get discouraged. Do not quit sowing seed, because some of the seed will land on good soil. When it does, it will yield an unbelievable harvest of exponential good.

Jesus concluded the parable of the four soils by saying, "Whoever has ears to hear, let them hear" (Mark 4:9). God wants to grow in our lives a great harvest of meaning, purpose, significance, and joy. This can happen for each one of us only if we keep the soil of our hearts soft and ready to welcome God's Word like a seed so it can do what comes so natural to it: Grow the good in us and through us.

A WINDOW, A MIRROR, AND AN INVITATION

Finishing the Stories of Jesus with Your Own Story

> A story is a way to say something that can't be said any other way.
>
> **FLANNERY O'CONNOR**

AS WE CLOSE, it is worth taking a step back from any specific, individual parable of Jesus to see what they all hold in common. Yes, they are "riddles thrown alongside" our lives. They have memorable characters, surprising twists, and profound meanings. And, of course, they are told by the master storyteller himself: Jesus. Beyond that, they are all also a window, a mirror, and an invitation.

A WINDOW INTO GOD'S KINGDOM

Jesus stories were down-to-earth ways to illustrate what the Kingdom of God is like. As Jesus said, "How can I describe the Kingdom of God? What story should I use to illustrate it?" (Mark 4:30, NLT). Jesus' parables can debunk myths we did not even know we believed, allowing us to see how the Kingdom actually works. They can heal disappointments we may develop from such misunderstandings of how God's Kingdom will function.

For example, if you think you have to possess a big faith to participate in God's Kingdom, you may be discouraged and disappointed until you hear that faith as small as a mustard seed or a bit of yeast will do. Similarly, we can fall into the trap of thinking that God's Kingdom comes in some magical way rather than through his work in giving people talents to manage for the good of the Kingdom. Expecting the wrong thing, we look in the wrong places. Jesus rights our expectations and grows our faith by the parables. We learn the very down-to-earth, everyday ways to participate in the Kingdom, including how to forgive, live in the mixture of good and evil, handle money and other resources, and celebrate when one person says yes to God. Through the parables, we get a picture of a God who is generous, just, forgiving, and searching for us as his beloved ones. We also discover that what we believe and the decisions we make in life really do matter.

A MIRROR INTO OUR OWN SOULS

The parables are not only a window into the Kingdom of God but also a mirror into our own hearts and souls. They are "thrown alongside" our lives to cause us to reflect on our lives. It is near impossible to hear the parables without asking ourselves where we fit within them. For example, when we hear the parable of the four soils, it's only natural to ask which soil most matches the condition of our own hearts. To hear the parable of the talents logically makes us take stock of what we are doing with what God has entrusted to us. The parable of the Good Samaritan forces us to answer the question of what kind of neighbor we will be to others. And the list goes on.

In fact, there are many more parables than I had space to address in this book. You can find a list of Jesus' twenty-nine parables (as well as where to locate them in the Bible) in the back of this book. From the parable of the sheep and goats to the story of the rich man and Lazarus, there are many parables that await your reflection. As with any mirror, sometimes we may be proud of what we see, while other times we may not. Regardless, the mirror's job is to give us a clear picture of ourselves.

AN INVITATION TO FINISH THE STORY IN OUR EVERYDAY LIVES

Ultimately, each of Jesus' down-to-earth stories is a window, a mirror, and an invitation given to us. Jesus did not come simply to tell these stories; he came to give us the power to change ours. He came to seek and save what is lost. The Bible is clear that we have all turned away from God in our own ways (see Romans 3:12). Jesus came to seek and save us. Me and you. The parables of the lost sheep, the lost coin, and the prodigal son are all told back to back to back by Jesus to drive home one point: He wants us to be reconciled to God. If we do this, it is reason for a great celebration in heaven.

How do we do this? By faith. The prodigal son had to trust in his father's goodness to want to return to him. It took some pain to get there, but it also took remembering his dad's scandalous grace. When he turned his trust into action, his father's grace was even beyond what he had the faith to believe: a robe, a ring, sandals, and a party for the child who had wanted nothing to do with his father.

We can have faith in God's goodness not just because of these stories but because of who is telling them. These parables would have been worthless had they been told by merely a traveling rabbi. But they are the greatest stories ever told because they are told by the one who died and rose again for us and our salvation. As with the merchant, Jesus bought us with a price because of his great love for us. When he did that, we are like the debtor who owed $7 billion dollars, only to have it forgiven by the generosity of the master.

Maybe you are reading this book and have never said yes to God, placing your hope and faith in him. You can do that now. Do not let the moment pass. Your life is too short and God's love for you too great for that. Here is a simple prayer you can pray (or use your own) if you want to say yes to Jesus' invitation:

Father, thank you for sending Jesus to give me a clear picture of your generosity, mercy, and goodness. Like the prodigal son, I have wandered off to a far country, but I want to come home. Please welcome me just like the father did for that younger son. Forgive me my debt because of what Jesus Christ has done on the cross to purchase me. Give me your Holy Spirit to change me from the inside out. Teach me from your Word, the Bible, so I may grow in joyfully following and obeying you all the days of my life. In Jesus' name, amen.

If you just made that decision to say yes to God for the first time, welcome to the family of God! As God's Word says speaking of Jesus, "To all who did receive him, to those who believed in his name, he gave the right to become children of God—children born not of natural descent, nor of human decision or a husband's will, but born of God" (John 1:12-13). Your next step is to join a local church that teaches the Bible. (I also invite you to listen to our weekly messages from Christian Assembly Church in Los Angeles at www.cachurch.com or on our iTunes podcast.)

Our relationship with God begins by hearing his invitation and saying yes by faith. But the invitation does not end there. We are invited to keep on saying yes in everyday ways as we live out our faith in action in every area of our lives. The yes of salvation is shown to be genuine by the everyday yes of discipleship. You can do it. God will help you (see Philippians 2:13). That is certainly part of what Jesus meant by his invitation to join God's Kingdom. N. T. Wright helps us see this:

> The cross has won the victory as a result of which there are now redeemed human beings getting ready to act as God's wise agents, his stewards, constantly worshiping their Creator and constantly, as a result, being equipped to reflect his image into his creation, to bring his wise and healing order to the world, putting the world to rights under his just and gentle rule.[1]

The parables make it clear that we are saved not just *from* something but also *for* something. God's Kingdom is like a celebration feast, and we are all invited. How we respond is up to us.

In fact, come to think of it, Jesus once told a parable about that.

ACKNOWLEDGMENTS

Down to Earth would never have been written without the involvement of some very supportive people. My wife Allison's encouragement for me to get away to write was the spark that got this project moving. Mark Pickerill's mentoring in my life cannot be overstated. Thank you, Mark. Thank you to the elders of Christian Assembly Church in Los Angeles who immediately saw this project as part of the ministry of Christian Assembly Church to the wider body of Christ. Thank you also to all the people who call Christian Assembly Church home. You have shaped the thoughts in this book through your efforts at joyfully following Jesus both here in Los Angeles and with our work all around the world. Without each of you, this book would never have been written.

Down to Earth would be a wholly diminished book without the efforts of some remarkably talented people. Don Pape's belief in this project as the publisher was the genesis of turning this idea into reality. David Zimmerman's editorial skills and tireless work have made this immeasurably better than when I gave it to him in manuscript form. Cara Iverson and Elizabeth Schroll both served to ensure that every *i* was dotted and *t* was crossed. Thank you also to the whole team at Tyndale House Publishers—including Dan Farrell, who designed the book's cover, and David Geeslin, for getting the word out about the book to as wide an audience as possible.

And to that stranger in England who picked me out of a group, telling me that one day, God would use my writing to go far beyond what I ever imagined: I guess the Lord really was speaking through you.

APPENDIX

The Parables of Jesus

PEOPLE DEBATE EXACTLY how many parables Jesus told. How you define a parable will depend on how many you end up with on your list. Here is a list of Jesus' twenty-nine parables with references from the Bible so you can consider even more of these "riddles thrown alongside" your life.

The Barren Fig Tree	Luke 13:6-9
The Budding Fig Tree	Matthew 24:32-35; Mark 13:28-31; Luke 21:29-33
The Dishonest Manager	Luke 16:1-9
The Friend at Night	Luke 11:5-8
The Good Samaritan	Luke 10:29-37
The Hidden Treasure	Matthew 13:44
The Lost Coin	Luke 15:8-10
The Lost Sheep	Matthew 18:10-14; Luke 15:3-7
The Mustard Seed	Matthew 13:31-32; Mark 4:30-32; Luke 13:18-19

The Net	Matthew 13:47-50
The Pearl of Great Value	Matthew 13:45-46
The Persistent Widow	Luke 18:1-8
The Pharisee and the Tax Collector	Luke 18:9-14
The Prodigal Son	Luke 15:11-32
The Rich Fool	Luke 12:16-21
The Rich Man and Lazarus	Luke 16:19-31
The Sheep and Goats	Matthew 25:31-46
The Sower	Matthew 13:1-9, 18-23; Mark 4:1-9, 13-20; Luke 8:4-8, 11-15
The Talents	Matthew 25:14-30; Luke 19:11-27
The Ten Bridesmaids	Matthew 25:1-13
The Tenants	Matthew 21:33-44; Mark 12:1-11; Luke 20:9-18
The Two Debtors	Luke 7:36-50
The Two Sons	Matthew 21:28-32
The Unforgiving Servant	Matthew 18:23-35
The Unjust Judge	Luke 18:1-8
The Great Banquet	Matthew 22:1-14; Luke 14:16-24
The Wedding Feast	Luke 14:7-14
The Weeds	Matthew 13:24-30, 36-43; Mark 4:26-29
The Yeast	Matthew 13:33; Luke 13:20-21

QUESTIONS FOR SMALL-GROUP DISCUSSION AND PERSONAL REFLECTION

CHAPTER 1: JESUS' MOST MISUNDERSTOOD PARABLES

1. Why do you think we tend to view ourselves as the merchant or the man in these stories rather than the pearl or the treasure?

2. Do you think of God's love as something you need to earn or as something God has already given to you apart from anything you have done? Why?

3. Of the four stages of spiritual development outlined by Bernard of Clairvaux, where do you see yourself currently? Why?

CHAPTER 2: A FRESH CHANCE FOR A FRESH START

1. Which of the two sons do you most relate to in this parable? Why?

2. What fresh choice is God inviting you to make as an act of getting in the wheelbarrow or going to the vineyard? Will you do it?

3. Who do you know who is still beating themselves up for pasts that are no longer true of them? What step can you take to share this parable of hope with them?

CHAPTER 3: THE STARTLING FORGIVENESS OF GOD

1. Have you asked for and experienced God's forgiveness for the debt you owe him for your sins? Why or why not?

2. If so, has that changed how you interact with others? Why or why not? How?

3. As a result of hearing this story, is there anyone God brings to mind that you are being invited to forgive in light of being forgiven?

CHAPTER 4: THE SECRET TO A STRONGER PRAYER LIFE

1. How does it change what Jesus is saying when you see that he is contrasting, not comparing, God with the neighbor?

2. The pagans viewed their gods as indifferent, bothered, or worn down by humans' disturbing prayer. Jesus came to give the true view that God is a loving, good, and generous Father, ready and willing to hear our prayers. Prior to hearing this parable, would you say your prayers reflected more of the pagan view of god or Jesus' view of God? Why?

3. What is one prayer request you have that you'd like the group to pray for this week? Or if doing this alone, what is something you would like to speak to God about, trusting that he will hear you? Go ahead and pray about that now.

4. Jesus concludes this parable by saying that we can even ask God the Father to give us his Holy Spirit. Have you ever simply taken Jesus at his word and asked to be given the Holy Spirit? If not, why not? I invite you to pray that simple prayer now, trusting in God's willingness to hear and respond to your request.

CHAPTER 5: MAXIMIZING WHAT YOU'VE BEEN GIVEN

1. What God-given talents do you believe (or have others told you) you have?

2. How does this parable make you feel when it comes to using the talents you've been given? Excited to jump in or afraid to make a mistake? Why?

3. In the parable, the faithful servants begin right away. What is something you can immediately do with the talents God has delegated to you for the sake of God's Kingdom and the good of others? Will you actually now go do it? Why or why not?

CHAPTER 6: THE SUREFIRE WAY TO ENSURE YOUR UNHAPPINESS

1. On a scale of 1 to 10 (1 being "none" and 10 being "a lot"), how much gratitude marks your everyday life? Why did you select that number?

2. Comparison is the thief of gratitude and joy. Is there anywhere in your life that you tend to compare yourself or your situation to others? How can you begin to change that pattern?

3. What is one thing you can do to limit the amount of negativity that comes your way, whether through the news, social media, or a chronically pessimistic person in your life?

4. Have you ever considered all the ways that life has been unfair in your favor? Take a moment to make a list of those ways.

CHAPTER 7: DOING FIRST WHAT MATTERS MOST

1. What are some regrets you have heard from people? What are some regrets you have realized about your own life?

2. What are some ways that God can redeem a person's past regrets?

3. How might Jesus' telling us this parable now be considered an act of grace?

4. What is God bringing to mind for you to do now so you do not regret *not* doing it later?

CHAPTER 8: THE JOY OF SPENDING SOMEONE ELSE'S MONEY

1. What is the most challenging part of this parable for you? Why?

2. Jesus did not warn people not to have money, but he did tell us not to serve money. What is the difference? As you take an honest look at your life, do you serve money?

3. What do you make of the owner commending the shrewd manager? Does that bother you or inspire you?

4. What is one thing you can do with the resources God has assigned to you, based on the message of this parable? Will you do it?

CHAPTER 9: WHY EVIL EXISTS NOW BUT WON'T FOREVER

1. Do you find comfort in the doctrine of divine judgment of evil? Why or why not?

2. What evil are you facing that you need to entrust to God's justice?

3. What evil do you need to pray for protection and deliverance from?

4. As you read this parable, does God bring to mind any evil that you are involved with that he is now calling you to stop and turn away from? If so, do that now.

CHAPTER 10: RISING HOPE IN TROUBLED TIMES

1. On a scale of 1 to 10 (with 1 being low and 10 being high), how hopeful of a person are you? What is one thing you can do to increase the amount of hope you experience each day?

2. How does having hope for the future affect your reality now?

3. Jesus told parables to encourage his listeners. Who is one person God may be asking you to encourage this week with a message of hope rooted in these parables?

CHAPTER 11: HOW TO BE A HERO

1. Jesus made a Samaritan the hero of the story that he told a group of people who generally hated Samaritans. Why

do you think he did that? How would you respond if Jesus exchanged the word *Samaritan* for any group that you are apt to dislike?

2. When it comes to loving your neighbor, do you find fear, time pressures, or skepticism to be your biggest obstacle to overcome? Why?

3. What is one thing you can do to love your neighbor through some tangible act? Will you do it?

CHAPTER 12: WELCOME HOME!

1. Which character do you most identify with in Jesus' parable? Why?

2. How has your view of God as the Father been influenced by your own father, stepfather, or other father figure?

3. What is God asking you to do or change as a result of this parable?

4. What is one thing you can do to be active, present, and merciful in the life of someone you love this week to reflect God's heart toward him or her?

CHAPTER 13: THE CREATIVE POTENTIAL OF A SOFT, DEEP, UNCLUTTERED HEART

1. Which of these four soils do you most relate to? Why?

2. Based on the soil that you selected, what do you think God is inviting you to pray about and do as a result of reading this parable?

3. God's Word is a seed to be planted in our hearts. What is one verse from the Bible that you are willing to memorize as a way of welcoming it into your heart? If you need some help thinking of one, try John 3:16, Ephesians 2:8-10, or Philippians 4:6.

4. Those who follow Christ are called to be sowers of God's Word. Who is God now prompting you to share his Word with? Will you do it?

CONCLUSION: A WINDOW, A MIRROR, AND AN INVITATION

1. Which of the fifteen parables did God most use to speak to you? Why?

2. What did you learn through these parables that surprised you the most when you think about the Kingdom of God? Why?

3. Of the list of Jesus' twenty-nine parables, which one are you most interested to read next? Why?

NOTES

INTRODUCTION: THE GREATEST STORIES EVER TOLD

1. As a translation of the Hebrew word מָשָׁל, *mashal*, the word *parable* refers to a riddle (https://biblehub.com/topical/s/sayings.htm). For examples of the word referring to a riddle, see Psalm 49:4-5, Psalm 78:2, and Proverbs 1:6.
2. Accordance Bible Software, version 9.6, Strong's Greek Lexicon, s.v. "3846. *paraballō*; to throw alongside," accessed December 6, 2018.
3. Helmut Thielicke, quoted in Haddon Robinson, "Seeing the Reflection in the Bible," *Preaching Today*, August 1997, https://www.preachingtoday.com /illustrations/1997/august/4687.html.
4. Alison Gopnik, "Want a Mind Meld? Tell a Compelling Story," *Wall Street Journal*, April 5, 2016.

CHAPTER 1: JESUS' MOST MISUNDERSTOOD PARABLES

1. F. Brown, S. Driver, and C. Briggs, *Brown-Driver-Briggs Hebrew and English Lexicon* (Accordance Bible Software, version 9.6: 2012).
2. "#207: Bernard of Clairvaux on Love," Christian History Institute, accessed December 7, 2018, https://christianhistoryinstitute.org/study/module/bernard.
3. See Luke 1:68 as translated in the New Living Translation, King James Version, and English Standard Version.
4. Walter Bauer, *A Greek-English Lexicon of the New Testament and Other Early Christian Literature* (Accordance Bible Software, version 9.6: 2012).

CHAPTER 2: A FRESH CHANCE FOR A FRESH START

1. Sean Gardiner, "In Name Game, Loser Wins and Brother Winner Loses," *Chicago Tribune*, July 31, 2002, http://articles.chicagotribune.com/2002-07-31 /news/0207310310_1_prep-school-burglary-case-criminal-justice-system.
2. Imagine Dragons, "Whatever It Takes."

3. My thanks to my friend Mark Pickerill for working with me on retelling this parable in a modern way.
4. Sean Strovas, in conversation with the author, May 2018.
5. Søren Kierkegaard, quoted in Leander E. Keck et al., *The New Interpreter's Bible Commentary: Hebrews–Revelation*, vol. 12 (Nashville: Abingdon, 1998), 391.
6. See "The Charles Blondin Story," Creative Bible Study, https://www.creativebible study.com/Blondin-story.html: "Later in August of 1859, his manager, Harry Colcord, did ride on Blondin's back across the Falls."

CHAPTER 3: THE STARTLING FORGIVENESS OF GOD
1. Kevin Jackson, "Christian Author Carries Mantle of the Woman She Killed," *Christian Post*, June 21, 2007, https://www.christianpost.com/news/christian -author-carries-mantle-of-the-woman-she-killed-28089/.
2. Philip Massey, "The Parable of the Two Debtors in Modern Terms," *The Chimes*, October 27, 2010, https://chimesnewspaper.com/13189/opinions/parable-two -debtors/.
3. Dietrich Bonhoeffer, quoted in Samuel C. Williamson, *Beliefs of the Heart* (blog), July 25, 2014, http://beliefsoftheheart.com/quotes/bonhoeffer-on -forgiveness/.
4. Massey, "Parable of the Two Debtors."
5. "Fred Craddock, in an Address to Ministers, Caught . . . ," *Sermon Central*, November 1, 2001, https://www.sermoncentral.com/sermon-illustrations/4425 /fred-craddock-in-an-address-to-ministers-caught-by-sermoncentral.
6. N. T. Wright, *Evil and the Justice of God* (Downers Grove, IL: IVP, 2013), 146–7.
7. Miroslav Volf, quoted in Michael Hidalgo, "The Pain of Forgiveness," *Sojourners* (blog), April 3, 2012, https://sojo.net/articles/pain-forgiveness.
8. "Mary Johnson and Oshea Israel," The Forgiveness Project, https://www .theforgivenessproject.com/mary-johnson-and-oshea-israel.
9. "Mary Johnson and Oshea Israel."
10. "Mary Johnson and Oshea Israel."
11. N. T. Wright, "Grasped by the Love of God," N. T. Wright Online, http:// ntwrightonline.org/grasped-love-god/.

CHAPTER 4: THE SECRET TO A STRONGER PRAYER LIFE
1. "Frequency of Prayer," Pew Research Center, http://www.pewforum.org/religious -landscape-study/frequency-of-prayer/. Daily prayer is self-reported by 55 percent of Americans; 47 percent of Americans have full-time employment: The Automatic Earth, "Only 47 Percent of Working Age Americans Have Full Time Jobs," *Business Insider*, January 24, 2011, http://www.businessinsider.com/real-employment-rate -47-percent-2011-1.
2. "Passion for Daily Prayer Grows with Age," *Preaching Today*, http://www.preaching today.com/illustrations/2010/may/3051010.html.

3. Owen Barfield, "Chronological Snobbery," Owen Barfield (website), http://www
.owenbarfield.org/chronological-snobbery/.

4. Smith Wigglesworth, quoted in Colin Dye, "Smith Wigglesworth on Prayer,"
Colin Dye (blog), March 4, 2013, http://www.colindye.com/2013/03/04/smith
-wigglesworth-on-prayer/.

5. Gladys Meggs, quoted in John Claypool, *Stories Jesus Still Tells: The Parables*
(Lanham: MD: Rowman & Littlefield, 2007), 108.

CHAPTER 5: MAXIMIZING WHAT YOU'VE BEEN GIVEN

1. Chuck Yeager, *Yeager: An Autobiography* (New York: Bantam, 1985), 234–5.

2. Yeager, 234.

3. "Can't Stop," track 7 on Red Hot Chili Peppers, *By the Way*, Warner Bros.,
2002.

4. Robert Louis Stevenson, *The Complete Works of Robert Louis Stevenson* (E-artnow,
2015), 2092.

5. Nick Vujicic, "Bio," Life without Limbs, https://www.lifewithoutlimbs.org/about
-nick/bio/.

6. Nick Vujicic, keynote address at Foursquare Connection, Seattle, Washington,
May 2018.

7. Oswald Chambers, *My Utmost for His Highest* (New York: Dodd, Mead, 1935),
July 13.

8. Andrew Murray, "Money II," *Christian History*, issue 19.

9. Howard Hendricks, "The Pithy Sayings of Beloved Howard Hendricks," June 17,
2013, *Enough Light*, https://lightenough.wordpress.com/2013/06/17/the-pithy
-sayings-of-beloved-howard-hendricks/.

10. Hendricks, "Pithy Sayings."

CHAPTER 6: THE SUREFIRE WAY TO ENSURE YOUR UNHAPPINESS

1. Theodore Roosevelt, Quote Fancy, https://quotefancy.com/quote/33048/Theodore
-Roosevelt-Comparison-is-the-thief-of-joy. (Although this quote is often attributed
to Roosevelt, some argue its origin.)

2. "Instagram's Envy Effect," *Relevant*, April 4, 2013, https://relevantmagazine.com
/article/stop-instagramming-your-perfect-life/.

3. D. A. Carson, *Exegetical Fallacies* (Grand Rapids, MI: Baker, 1996), 22.

4. Aleksandr Solzhenitsyn, Goodreads, https://www.goodreads.com/quotes/415498
-what-about-the-main-thing-in-life-all-its.

5. John Claypool, *Stories Jesus Still Tells: The Parables* (Lanham: MD: Rowman &
Littlefield, 2007), 28.

6. Claypool, *Stories*, 32.

7. Claypool, *Stories*, 32–33.

8. "The 31 Benefits of Gratitude You Didn't Know About: How Gratitude Can
Change Your Life," *Happier Human* (blog), https://happierhuman.com/benefits
-of-gratitude/.

9. Max Lucado, *Anxious for Nothing: Finding Calm in a Chaotic World* (Nashville: Thomas Nelson, 2017), 94.

10. Dallas Willard, *The Great Omission: Reclaiming Jesus's Essential Teachings on Discipleship* (New York: HarperCollins, 2014), 61.

CHAPTER 7: DOING FIRST WHAT MATTERS MOST

1. Jordan Zaslow, "We Asked People to Tell Us Their Biggest Regrets—But What They All Had in Common Was Heartbreaking," *A Plus*, January 22, 2016, https://aplus.com/a/clean-slate-blackboard-experiment?no_monetization=true.

2. C. S. Lewis, "First and Second Things," C. S. Lewis Institute, July 2017, http://www.cslewisinstitute.org/First_and_Second_Things.

3. William Willimon, "Will Willimon Learns Hard Truth at Funeral," *Preaching Today*, https://www.preachingtoday.com/illustrations/2009/january/6012609.html.

4. Willimon, "Will Willimon Learns Hard Truth."

5. R. C. Sproul, *The Holiness of God* (Carol Stream, IL: Tyndale, 2000), 129.

6. Zaslow, "Biggest Regrets."

CHAPTER 8: THE JOY OF SPENDING SOMEONE ELSE'S MONEY

1. "Statistic: Jesus' Teachings on Money," *Preaching Today*, https://www.preachingtoday.com/illustrations/1996/december/410.html.

2. *Merriam-Webster*, s.v. "tithe (*n.*)," https://www.merriam-webster.com/dictionary/tithe.

3. Brian Dodd, "Generous Church: Ten Top Characteristics," Church Leaders, May 31, 2011, https://churchleaders.com/pastors/pastor-how-to/151049-brian-dodd-generous-church-ten-top-characteristics.html.

4. Dodd, "Generous Church."

5. Dodd, "Generous Church."

CHAPTER 9: WHY EVIL EXISTS NOW BUT WON'T FOREVER

1. Max Lucado, "This Evil Will Not Last Forever," Max Lucado (website), https://maxlucado.com/this-evil-will-not-last-forever/.

2. Miroslav Volf, *Exclusion and Embrace: A Theological Exploration of Identity, Otherness, and Reconciliation* (Nashville: Abingdon, 1996), 303–4.

3. Norman L. Geisler and Ronald M. Brooks, *When Skeptics Ask: A Handbook on Christian Evidences* (Grand Rapids, MI: Baker, 2013), 67.

4. Volf, *Exclusion and Embrace*, 304.

5. Ravi Zacharias, "Think Again," RZIM, https://rzim.org/just-thinking/think-again-2/.

6. Aleksandr Solzhenitsyn, Goodreads, https://www.goodreads.com/author/quotes/10420.Aleksandr_Solzhenitsyn.

CHAPTER 10: RISING HOPE IN TROUBLED TIMES

1. Wikipedia, s.v. "Florence Chadwick," last modified July 3, 2018, 17:23, https://en.wikipedia.org/wiki/Florence_Chadwick.
2. Florence Chadwick, quoted in Randy Alcorn, "Florence Chadwick and the Fog," Eternal Perspective Ministries, January 21, 2010, https://www.epm.org/resources/2010/Jan/21/florence-chadwick-and-fog/.
3. Samantha McMullen, "What Is the Size of a Mustard Bush?" *SFGate*, December 29, 2018, http://homeguides.sfgate.com/size-mustard-bush-100618.html.

CHAPTER 11: HOW TO BE A HERO

1. David Usborne, "Subway Hero: 'I Had to Decide, Do I Let the Train Run Him Over,'" *Independent*, January 4, 2007, https://www.independent.co.uk/news/world/americas/subway-hero-i-had-to-decide-do-i-let-the-train-run-him-over-430718.html.
2. Usborne, "Subway Hero."
3. John Wilkinson, "The Way from Jerusalem to Jericho," *Biblical Archaeologist* 38, no. 1 (March 1975): 10–24.
4. J. M. Darley and C. D. Batson, "From Jerusalem to Jericho: A Study of Situational and Dispositional Variables in Helping Behavior," *Journal of Personality and Social Psychology* 27 (1973): 100–108, http://faculty.babson.edu/krollag/org_site/soc_psych/darley_samarit.html.
5. Dallas Willard, quoted in John Ortberg, "Ruthlessly Eliminate Hurry," *Christianity Today*, https://www.christianitytoday.com/pastors/2002/july-online-only/cln20704.html.
6. John Claypool, *Stories*, 95.
7. N. T. Wright, *Evil and the Justice of God* (Downers Grove, IL: IVP, 2013), 161.
8. *Love Does* is the great title of a book written by Bob Goff (Nashville: Thomas Nelson, 2012).
9. Martin Luther, quoted in Rich Nathan, "The Grace of Being Tender-Hearted," *Preaching Today*, July 2013, https://www.preachingtoday.com/sermons/sermons/2013/july/grace-of-being-tender-hearted.html.
10. "Mission, Vision and Values," Ascension, https://www.ascension.org/Our-Mission/Mission-Vision-Values.
11. Joseph Sunde, "The Halo Effect: The Economic Value of the Local Church," *Acton Institute* (blog), July 20, 2016, http://blog.acton.org/archives/88116-the-halo-effect-the-economic-value-of-the-local-church.html.
12. Fred B. Craddock, *Luke: Interpretation: A Bible Commentary for Teaching and Preaching* (Louisville, KY: John Knox, 2009), 192.

CHAPTER 12: WELCOME HOME!

1. This story is recounted by Richard Carol Hoefler, and is found in Curtis E. Liens, *The Man with Dirty Hands* (self-published, 2000).
2. "Faith of the Fatherless," beliefnet, accessed December 12, 2018, https://www.beliefnet.com/love-family/2000/06/faith-of-the-fatherless.aspx.

3. Josh McDowell, "Finding Freedom in the Truth: Josh and Sean McDowell," Jesus Calling, podcast, https://www.jesuscalling.com/blog/finding-freedom-truth -josh-sean-mcdowell/.

4. Jonathan Petersen, "The Undeniable Reliability of Scripture: An Interview with Josh McDowell," November 11, 2015, https://www.biblegateway.com/blog /2015/11/the-undeniable-reliability-of-scripture-an-interview-with-josh -mcdowell/.

5. *Merriam-Webster*, s.v. "prodigal (*adj.*)," https://www.merriam-webster.com/dictionary /prodigal.

6. "Whatever It Takes," track 2 on Imagine Dragons, *Evolve*, Interscope, 2017.

7. Henri J. M. Nouwen, *The Return of the Prodigal Son: A Story of Homecoming* (New York: Doubleday, 1994), 42–43.

8. C. S. Lewis, *The Problem of Pain* (New York: HarperOne, 2015), 91.

9. Matt Williams, "The Prodigal Son's Father Shouldn't Have Run!" *Biola Magazine*, summer 2010, http://magazine.biola.edu/article/10-summer/the-prodigal-sons -father-shouldnt-have-run/.

CHAPTER 13: THE CREATIVE POTENTIAL OF A SOFT, DEEP, UNCLUTTERED HEART

1. "Mosquito Targets Teens with Audio Repellent," interview by Neal Conan, Talk of the Nation, NPR, September 1, 2010, https://www.npr.org/templates/story /story.php?storyId=129581152.

2. See "Musical Note to Frequency Conversion Chart," accessed December 12, 2018, https://www.audiology.org/sites/default/files/ChasinConversionChart.pdf.

3. John Donovan, "Most People over 18 Can't Hear These Sounds," Mnn.com, July 24, 2015, https://www.mnn.com/health/fitness-well-being/stories/most -people-over-18-cant-hear-these-sounds.

4. Paul Vitello, "A Ring Tone Meant to Fall on Deaf Ears," *New York Times*, June 12, 2006, https://www.nytimes.com/2006/06/12/technology/12ring.html.

5. Stephanie Leach, addressing Christian Assembly Church, May 2018.

6. *Boston Collaborative Encyclopedia of Western Theology*, s.v. "Wolfhart Pannenberg," http://people.bu.edu/wwildman/bce/pannenberg.htm.

7. Wolfhart Pannenberg, conversation with Ron Sider, *Prism Magazine* (March/April 1997).

8. Robbie Conal, quoted in Sarah Linn, "Robbie Conal: Meet the Godfather of Guerrilla Street Art," KCET, February 16, 2016, https://www.kcet.org/shows /artbound/robbie-conal-street-art.

9. Richard Foster, quoted in Nathan Foster, "The Cure for Distraction: Staying Present through Intentional Slowing," *Renovaré*, July 24, 2018, https://renovare .org/articles/the-cure-for-distraction.

CONCLUSION: A WINDOW, A MIRROR, AND AN INVITATION

1. Wright, *Evil and the Justice of God* (Downers Grove, IL: IVP, 2013), 139.

ABOUT THE AUTHOR

TOM HUGHES grew up in Pittsburgh, Pennsylvania. After studying sociology, environmental studies, and world religions at Ohio Wesleyan University, he was headed to Ohio State law school when God redirected him to become a pastor. He launched and led a student ministry on the East Coast before moving to England to study with the missional-church movement. Tom then moved to Los Angeles to earn his master of divinity degree at Fuller Theological Seminary.

Tom and his wife, Allison, were invited by a neighbor to Christian Assembly Church in 2002. In 2003, Tom joined the Christian Assembly staff as part of the teaching team with the specific assignment to reach young adults. In 2007, Tom became the co-lead pastor there. Christian Assembly has grown to include twenty-five gospel-centered partnerships active in fifteen countries. The work ranges from a hospice-care ministry to strengthening the persecuted church to mentoring at-risk children in public schools to planting churches in Los Angeles to ministering to unreached people groups, and much more. Tom is also the author of *Curious: The Unexpected Power of a Question-Led Life*, which explores how Jesus' questions can change our lives. You can learn more about Christian Assembly, including hearing Tom's weekend messages, at www.cachurch.com. You can also find the *Down to Earth* and *Curious* devotional Bible-reading plans on the YouVersion Bible App.

Tom is a rabid Pittsburgh Steelers fan who loves the mountains and still enjoys kicking a soccer ball around from time to time. He and Allison have three delightful children: Caleb, Sophia, and Micah.